40 Active Learning Strategies

for the Inclusive Classroom

Grades K–5

Linda Schwartz Green
Diane Casale-Giannola

Foreword by Toby J. Karten

CORWIN
A SAGE Company

For information:

Corwin
A SAGE Company
2455 Teller Road
Thousand Oaks, California 91320
www.corwin.com

SAGE Ltd.
1 Oliver's Yard
55 City Road
London, EC1Y 1SP
United Kingdom

SAGE Pvt. Ltd.
B 1/I 1 Mohan Cooperative
    Industrial Area
Mathura Road, New Delhi 110 044
India

SAGE Asia-Pacific Pte. Ltd.
33 Pekin Street #02-01
Far East Square
Singapore 048763

Printed in the United States of America

Library of Congress Cataloging-in-Publication Data

Green, Linda Schwartz, author.
40 active learning strategies for the inclusive classroom, grades K-5 / Linda Schwartz Green, Diane Casale-Giannola ; Foreword by Toby J. Karten.
    p. cm
Includes bibliographical references.
ISBN 978-1-4129-8170-5 (pbk.)

   1. Active learning. 2. Activity programs in education. 3. Education (Elementary). 4. Inclusive education. I. Casale-Giannola, Diane, author. II. Title. III. Title: Forty active learning strategies for the inclusive classroom, grades K-5.

LB1027.23.G738 2011
371.9'046—dc22   2010044641

This book is printed on acid-free paper.

11 12 13 14 15 10 9 8 7 6 5 4 3 2 1

Acquisitions Editor:	Jessica Allan
Associate Editor:	Allison Scott
Editorial Assistant:	Lisa Whitney
Production Editor:	Veronica Stapleton
Copy Editor:	Diana Breti
Typesetter:	C&M Digitals (P) Ltd.
Proofreader:	Dennis W. Webb
Cover Designer:	Michael Dubowe
Permissions Editor:	Karen Ehrmann

Contents

Foreword

Educators must ensure that students who enter classroom environments are welcomed with appropriate pedagogical approaches that match their diverse needs. We have, thankfully, entered a new century of learning in which classrooms include students of all abilities. Inclusion is not a fad; it is an ongoing philosophy that invites and prepares children to prosper beyond classroom walls into accepting societies. It is obvious from the contents of this book, *40 Active Learning Strategies for the Inclusive Classroom, Grades K–5,* that our authors, Dr. Linda Schwartz Green and Dr. Diane Casale-Giannola, are firm believers in the application of effective inclusive classroom practices.

Their book outlines ways for teachers to creatively deliver the curriculum. As the pages unfold, you will discover palatable strategies that allow students to enthusiastically ingest the educational experiences while being active learners. The authors have addressed learners' emotional and academic characteristics with quality-leveled differentiated instruction. Terms such as brain-based learning, differentiated instruction, and information processing come alive through the vignettes, step-by-step directions, activities, and reflections. The text steers students and teachers in the direction of learning for retention with active strategies that connect to both the concepts and individual learners.

Creating inclusive classrooms can be an undertaking fit for Sisyphus if you allow yourself to be dissuaded by the enormity of the goal. However, the authors have simplified this task for educators of primary grade students. During their years of experience in the field of special education, they have accumulated an array of active learning strategies that support the unique needs of learners in inclusive environments. The applicable strategies convey the curriculum to students' minds by engaging the children with fun learning experiences to solidify the knowledge. At the same time, educators are then equipped with motivating ways to teach. This active engagement translates to higher retention and, ultimately, achievements across the curriculum for students in inclusive classrooms.

Education was never a one-size-fits-all approach because learners have always exhibited diversity in prior knowledge, abilities, motivation, and preferred styles of learning. However, resources such as this text were not always readily available. Differentiation of instruction requires that teachers have strategies such as these at their fingertips. In this fast-paced world, we as educators need to honor students' learning characteristics and, at the same time, make them smile while they learn. *40 Active Learning Strategies for the Inclusive Classroom, Grades K–5,* accomplishes just that!

Toby J. Karten

Acknowledgments

The writing of this book was an equal partnership, and we acknowledge one another for our devotion, patience, expertise, and humor. We realize how lucky we are to work so well together on such a meaningful project.

We acknowledge Dr. Michele Wilson Kamens, true friend and colleague, for her support and collaborative spirit that brought us together. We recognize Dr. James Patterson, a true magician, for making things reappear. A major thank you to Sandra Genduso, for going above and beyond.

We would like to acknowledge Centenary College and Rider University for their support in our professional and creative endeavors, not the least of which was the opportunity to write this book. It is most important to recognize our students throughout the years, from pre-K through college, whose enthusiastic participation has inspired us to write this book. We gratefully acknowledge our current and former students, the undergraduate and graduate students from Rider University and Centenary College. To all of you, thanks for the enthusiasm with which you participated, the energy you brought to our classes, and the feedback you shared with us; we are so glad that you tried out our strategies with your own students, during practicum or student teaching or in your own classrooms.

We thank Corwin for giving us the opportunity to share our contributions with so many. We truly appreciate our editor, Jessica Allan, for her enthusiasm and encouragement. She has been a tremendous asset throughout this process. Allison Scott answered question after question after question with patience and grace; we thank you.

The purpose of this book is to reach out to the educators in today's classroom, those of you who will take our ideas and go forth and meet the needs of all your students; we appreciate your willingness to try new things and your dedication to your students.

Finally, we thank our families for their love, support, and patience throughout this process; we couldn't have done it without you!

PUBLISHER'S ACKNOWLEDGMENTS

Corwin wishes to acknowledge the following peer reviewers for their editorial insight and guidance.

Donna Adkins
Teacher
Perritt Primary
Arkadelphia, AR

Rachel Aherns
Instructional Strategist I
Westridge Elementary
West Des Moines, IA

Jim Hoogheem
Retired Principal
Osseo Area Schools
Maple Grove, MN

Rui Kang
Assistant Professor
Georgia College & State University
Milledgeville, GA

Cheryl Moss
Special Education Teacher
Gilbert Middle School
Ames, IA

Patti Palmer
Sixth Grade Language Arts Teacher
Wynford School
Bucyrus, OH

Amanda M. Rudolph
Associate Professor
Stephen F. Austin State University
Nacogdoches, TX

About the Authors

 **Linda Schwartz Green** has been involved in the field of special education since the beginning of her career, teaching in public school, starting the first resource room in her district, and working as a liaison between school and family before becoming a faculty member at Centenary College. As her children were growing up and people asked what their mom did, the response was always "She teaches teachers how to teach." That pretty much sums it up. She is the director of the Students with Disabilities certification program, created the MA in Special Education, and serves as director of the special education graduate program. She received the Centenary College Distinguished Teacher Award. Dr. Green has also been an educational consultant, preparing and implementing numerous workshops on a variety of topics related to special education for teachers and for parents, and she regularly presents at national special education conferences.

She received her undergraduate degree in English and English Education from the University of Bridgeport, an MA in Special Education and Reading from Eastern New Mexico University, and a PhD in Special Education and Psychological and Cultural Studies from the University of Nebraska. Growing up in New York City and continuing her education in Connecticut, New Mexico, and Nebraska sparked not only her love of learning but also the quest to visit every state in the union (only four more to go).

 **Diane Casale-Giannola** is a dedicated educator. She has taught preschool to graduate school. She is a native New Yorker who has a passion for culture and international experiences and has taught in the United States and abroad. She has also worked in many leadership roles, including assistant principal, director, and principal. Diane has several degrees, including a BA in English and Secondary Education and a MSc in Special Education from the State University of New York at Albany, an Advanced Certificate in Education Administration and Supervision from Brooklyn College, and a PhD in Education Administration and Leadership from New York University.

Currently a faculty member of Rider University, Diane Casale-Giannola has been recognized as the Distinguished Teacher of the Year. Other educational endeavors include professional development, consulting, and speaking at educational conferences nationally and internationally. Her research interests and publications focus on supporting diverse learners through inclusion, global education, and effective practice. Diane is committed to lifelong learning and believes the recipe for success in education is one part knowledge, one part organization, one part passion, and two parts humor. Diane is committed to making a difference in the lives of others and improving a diverse world.

This book is dedicated to the most important people in my life:
to my husband and fellow traveler, Marc, for always believing in me and making me laugh.
You seem to know what I can accomplish before I do. Our adventure continues!
to Jessica and Adam: being your Mom made me a better educator,
and to Nia: so glad to have you as part of the family. Thanks to all three of you for your support
throughout this project and for always helping me to remember what is really important.

Linda Schwartz Green

This book is dedicated to my three wonderful children, Victoria, Christian, and Francesca;
when asked who is their favorite teacher, they respond, "Mommy!" You all make
me proud and keep life interesting! And to my mother, Ann Casale,
for her love and support.

Diane Casale-Giannola

Engaging Students in the Inclusive Classroom

Research and Theoretical Underpinning

THE BLUEBERRY STORY: THE TEACHER
GIVES THE BUSINESSMAN A LESSON

"If I ran my business the way you people operate your schools, I wouldn't be in business very long!"

I stood before an auditorium filled with outraged teachers who were becoming angrier by the minute. My speech had entirely consumed their precious 90 minutes of inservice. Their initial icy glares had turned to restless agitation. You could cut the hostility with a knife.

I represented a group of business people dedicated to improving public schools. I was an executive at an ice cream company that became famous in the middle 1980s when *People Magazine* chose our blueberry as the "Best Ice Cream in America."

I was convinced of two things. First, public schools needed to change; they were archaic selecting and sorting mechanisms designed for the industrial age and out of step with the needs of our emerging "knowledge society." Second, educators were a major part of the problem: they resisted change, hunkered down in their feathered nests, protected by tenure and shielded by a bureaucratic monopoly. They needed to look to business. We knew how to produce quality. Zero defects! TQM! Continuous improvement!

(Continued)

(Continued)

In retrospect, the speech was perfectly balanced—equal parts ignorance and arrogance.

As soon as I finished, a woman's hand shot up. She appeared polite, pleasant—she was, in fact, a razor-edged, veteran, high school English teacher who had been waiting to unload.

She began quietly, "We are told, sir, that you manage a company that makes good ice cream."

I smugly replied, "Best ice cream in America, Ma'am."

"How nice," she said. "Is it rich and smooth?"

"Sixteen percent butterfat," I crowed.

"Premium ingredients?" she inquired.

"Super-premium! Nothing but triple A." I was on a roll. I never saw the next line coming.

"Mr. Vollmer," she said, leaning forward with a wicked eyebrow raised to the sky, "when you are standing on your receiving dock and you see inferior shipments of blueberries arrive, what do you do?"

In the silence of that room, I could hear the trap snap. . . . I was dead meat, but I wasn't going to lie.

"I send them back."

"That's right!" she barked, "and we can never send back our blueberries. We take them big, small, rich, poor, gifted, exceptional, abused, frightened, confident, homeless, rude, and brilliant. We take them with ADHD, junior rheumatoid arthritis, and English as their second language. We take them all! Every one! And that, Mr. Vollmer, is why it's not a business. It's school!"

In an explosion, all 290 teachers, principals, bus drivers, aides, custodians, and secretaries jumped to their feet and yelled, "Yeah! Blueberries! Blueberries!"

And so began my long transformation.

Since then, I have visited hundreds of schools. I have learned that a school is not a business. Schools are unable to control the quality of their raw material, they are dependent upon the vagaries of politics for a reliable revenue stream, and they are constantly mauled by a howling horde of disparate, competing customer groups that would send the best CEO screaming into the night.

None of this negates the need for change. We must change what, when, and how we teach to give all children maximum opportunity to thrive in a post-industrial society. But educators cannot do this alone; these changes can occur only with the understanding, trust, permission, and active support of the surrounding community. For the most important thing I have learned is that schools reflect the attitudes, beliefs, and health of the communities they serve, and therefore, to improve public education means more than changing our schools, it means changing America.

This true story speaks to the very heart of education: It is our job; our responsibility; and our ethical, moral, and professional obligation to educate every one of the children who come through our doors. Teachers work to maximize the potential in every child. How to best accomplish this is the issue.

Inclusion, differentiated instruction, learning styles, learning modalities, multiple intelligences, and blueberries! Different concepts related to a common goal. Diverse students are included in our classrooms, and teachers need a variety of methods and strategies to support students' strengths and address their needs. Inclusion teachers need to be equipped with the expertise and strategies to motivate students and enhance student performance and learning outcomes.

The very best teachers share ideas, pool their resources, and are always looking for another creative way to structure a lesson or to motivate a reluctant learner. It is impossible for any one person to possess the knowledge, ability, and creativity to meet the needs of every child in the classroom, but each of us continues to strive toward this goal. Teachers consistently seek out methods that will positively affect student growth. This book is one such resource that will build your repertoire of strategies to support and engage students of varying needs and ages in the inclusion elementary school classroom. Please take this journey with us.

INCLUSION: DEFINITION AND RESEARCH

Inclusion is the term used to describe the education of students with disabilities in general education settings (Mastropieri & Scruggs, 2000). Inclusion is based on the philosophy that all students with a disability have a right to be educated in the general education setting with appropriate support and services to enable them to succeed. Accountability no longer lies with the special educator alone (Smith, Palloway, Patton, & Dowdy, 2006). Inclusion recognizes that all students are learners who benefit from a meaningful, challenging, and appropriate curriculum and differentiated instruction techniques that address their unique strengths and needs (Salend, 2005). Inclusion education is the collaborative effort of general educators, parents, related-service providers, and all school community members who share a role in the successful education of students with special needs.

Salend (2005) and Smith et al. (2006) summarize the advantages of inclusion: Research indicates that at the elementary school level, students with disabilities who are included in general education curricula can benefit socially and academically without facing the stigma of segregated or pull-out classrooms. Standards for behavior and instruction are higher, and students with classifications have more opportunity to reach higher standards and become independent learners.

Studies also indicate that students without disabilities can benefit from inclusive settings. Findings reveal academic performance is equal or superior to comparative groups of students educated in a noninclusive setting, and students with severe disabilities do not significantly limit or interrupt instructional time for nondisabled peers in inclusive settings. Friendships and awareness of diversity are also benefits of the inclusive classroom for individuals without disabilities.

STUDENTS IN THE INCLUSIVE CLASSROOM: WHO ARE WE TEACHING?

The inclusive classroom includes students with and without disabilities. Diverse student learners are identified, and the characteristics of learners are considered in the planning and instructional process. Students with special education classifications, served under the Individuals with Disabilities Act (IDEA), include children with the following classifications: autism, communication disorders, deaf-blindness, hearing impairments, other health impairments, emotional disabilities, specific learning disabilities, cognitive impairments, traumatic brain injuries, and visual impairments. Other instances of classroom diversity not associated with disabilities but important in the inclusive academic and social learning experience are cultural and linguistic diversity, such as English Language Learners; at-risk students, such as students with sociocultural disadvantages and limited experiences; gifted and talented students; and students who exhibit specific skills or abilities substantially above others of their age and grade level. Even without a classification, "average" students come to the classroom with unique abilities, needs, and interests. Blueberries *all* of them; none turned away!

HELPING TEACHERS MEET THE INCLUSION CHALLENGE

Although general education teachers typically support the concept of inclusive education, they often find themselves unsupported and ill-equipped to provide effective instruction and support for diverse students in the inclusive classroom (Bender, 2008; Mastropieri & Scruggs, 2000). Teachers are often "hungry" for strategies to support students with disabilities in the general education classroom (Bender, 2008). Even when teachers have a positive attitude toward inclusion, knowledge of how to adapt instruction, and the desire to make instructional changes, they still do not significantly alter their traditional whole group instructional approaches (Friend & Bursuck, 2002). As co-teaching becomes more common in the inclusive classroom, two teachers have even more opportunity to provide "unique and high-involvement instructional strategies to engage all students in ways that are not possible when only one teacher is present" (p. 110). Such creative options will enhance learning for all students, not just those with disabilities (Friend, 2010).

Active learning is a viable option that can accommodate diverse student needs in the inclusive classroom, meeting student and curricula challenges (Udvari-Solner & Kluth, 2008). Brain-based learning and motivational research support such strategies because they provide opportunities to engage students in the learning process. Active learning strategies can be instrumental in the teacher's quest to create positive learning experiences and outcomes.

This book provides an opportunity for teachers to explore a multitude of active learning strategies that will support students academically and socially in inclusive settings.

WHAT IS ACTIVE LEARNING?

To clarify our terms, we have developed our own working definition of active learning:

> Active learning is the intentional opportunity for students to engage in the learning process. It connects learners to the content through movement, reflection, or discussion, making students the center of the learning

process as they take the initiative to learn. It can be behavioral and/or cognitive, supporting a variety of instructional objectives from recall through synthesis.

Silberman (1996) addresses the question of what makes learning active. He explains, "When learning is active, students do most of the work. They use their brains, study ideas, solve problems, and apply what they learn. Active learning is fast-paced, fun, supportive, and personally engaging" (p. ix). Often students are out of their seats, moving about, and thinking aloud. Active learning engages and motivates students while enhancing understanding and performance (Guillaume, Yopp, & Yopp, 2007; Silberman, 1996, 2006; Udvari-Solner & Kluth, 2008; Zmuda, 2008). It is important to make learning active because to learn something well, a student needs to hear it, see it, ask questions about it, and discuss it with others. Above all, students need to do it (Silberman, 1996).

Research studies report that many active learning strategies are equally effective for mastering content when compared to the lecture format; what is significant is that active learning strategies are superior to lectures for student achievement in thinking and writing.

Cognitive research also supports the premise that student learning styles are best addressed with multiple instructional methodologies (Bonwell & Eisen, 1991). Bonwell and Eisen, educators who popularized the term *active learning*, describe its general characteristics as follows:

- Students are involved in more than listening.
- Instruction emphasizes the development of students' skill rather than just transmitting information.
- Students develop higher-order thinking skills (analysis, synthesis, evaluation).
- Students are engaged in activities (e.g., reading, discussing, writing).
- Students explore their own attitudes and values.

Pedagogy that includes interactive teaching strategies leads to education for sustainable learning (Corney & Reid, 2007). Teachers who embrace experiential learning can use active or hands-on experiences as methods to recognize desirable outcomes and endorse student-centered instructional approaches (Fenwick, 2001). Research has confirmed that student-centered, hands-on experiences improve construction of knowledge, comprehension, and the retention of content information.

Active learning strategies can support all levels of objectives in Bloom's taxonomy, from knowledge and translation to evaluation and synthesis. Active learning is particularly important for application, which is necessary for learning to transfer from short-term to long-term memory and be easily retrievable. Jarolimek and Foster (1981) describe the "activity mode" of teaching as a set of strategies that involves students in learning by doing things that are meaningful and related to the topic of study. Techniques include role playing, constructing, interpreting, preparing exhibits, processing, group work, and games. Active learning may also apply to inquiry modes of learning, which include such techniques as drawing conclusions, asking questions, and stating hypotheses (J. Wood, 2009). The strategies shared in *this* book are designed to actively engage students in their own learning. Alone they are activities, but once the activity is connected to specific learning and behavioral objectives, they become strategies to support learners and achievement outcomes. This active learning concept relates directly to the Native American proverb, "I hear and I forget; I see and I remember; I do and I understand" (J. Wood, 2009).

BRAIN-BASED LEARNING

Brain imaging devices can now give researchers a look inside the brain and determine which areas are involved as it carries out certain tasks. Some of these discoveries are valuable for diagnosing medical problems, while others have implications for what educators do in schools and classrooms. (Sousa, 2007)

William Bender (2002) lists 10 tactics for a brain-compatible classroom, based on the accumulated research in this area, including the following:

- structure frequent student responses,
- pair physical movement to learning tasks,
- use visual stimuli for increasing novelty in the learning task,
- give students choices, and
- use students to teach each other. (p. 26)

Clearly, using active learning strategies that involve children directly in their own learning is compatible with what we are learning about brain function. These strategies can help to differentiate instruction and support students with and without disabilities in the classroom (Bender, 2008). Many of these strategies involve movement, which can cause the brain to release dopamine and noradrenalin, neurotransmitters that help learners feel better, increase energy levels, and assist their brain to store and retrieve information (Jensen, 2000).

INFORMATION PROCESSING

Figure 1.1 Information Processing Model

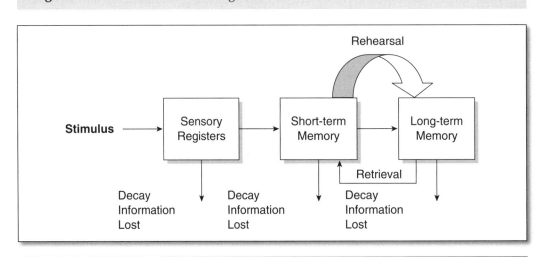

Source: Swanson (1987).

Information processing refers to how people learn new content. The information processing model, Figure 1.1, "is an attempt to describe how sensory input is perceived, transformed, reduced, elaborated, stored, retrieved, and used" (Swanson, 1987). The stimulus is perceived by sensory registers and transferred to short-term memory. At this point, there is rehearsal of new content in order for it to be transferred to long-term memory, from which it can be retrieved (Sliva, 2004). Simply stated, learners have to do something with new information to keep it in short-term memory or transfer it to long-term memory in a meaningful way, so that it can be retrieved as needed.

Think about a junk drawer you may have in your house. (Doesn't everybody have at least one in the kitchen where keys, pens, and all kinds of small objects are jumbled together?) Compare this to your silverware drawer, where each item has a place. In which drawer is it easier to find what you need quickly? Organization facilitates retrieval. In the same way, new information needs to be held in short-term memory, or transferred from short-term memory to long-term memory, in an organized manner so that the student can find and retrieve this information easily.

> If information is to be learned, it will either be transferred to and stored in long-term memory, or a strategy will be utilized to keep the information in short-term memory. Unless a strategy is used to remember this information, it will be lost in about 15 seconds. Some strategies that can be utilized to keep this information active in short-term memory are to rehearse the information, chunk it, elaborate on it, or create visual images of it. Information is then transferred from short-term memory to long-term memory where it is stored until needed. (Sliva, 2004, p. 16)

Rehearsing the information refers to going over it more than once. *Chunking* it refers to dividing the information into smaller pieces or sections and studying each section. We can also chunk information in sections that relate to one another. When we *elaborate on* new content, we describe it in more depth, often relating it to prior knowledge. *Creating a visual image* of new content can include pictures, symbols, or diagrams to help us remember.

The important point is that in order to fully learn new information, we have to become involved with the learning process, utilizing one or more strategies to promote understanding and keep the material in short-term memory or facilitate meaningful storage in long-term memory. Information processing generally takes place both unconsciously and automatically. As learners, we are not always cognizant of how and when the procedure takes place (Sliva, 2004). As educators, it is important for us to be aware of this process and of how we can design instruction that encourages successful information processing. Including active learning strategies in instructional design is one way to accomplish this.

CONNECTIONS TO DIFFERENTIATED INSTRUCTION

Differentiated instruction provides multiple opportunities to support diverse students in inclusive settings. It requires teachers to identify the strengths and needs of their students and possess a repertoire of strategies to support students with and without disabilities. It challenges teachers to study and think about the learning process as they find avenues to engage and motivate diverse students. It takes into account individuals' needs, readiness, interests, and learning profiles. It focuses on instruction that appeals to and engages each student (King-Shaver & Hunter, 2003).

Interest refers to curiosity and passion for a specific topic, while *learning profile* refers to a student's intelligence preferences, gender, and learning style (Tomlinson, 1999). Teachers must be ready to engage students in instruction using different learning modalities (visual, auditory, kinesthetic, or tactile), appealing to interests and degrees of complexity. Differentiated instruction focuses on the content, product, and process of learning (Tomlinson, 1999).

"The apparent differences in how children learn should be used as a basis for planning instruction" (Tomlinson, 1999). When choosing activities that will engage and include students, purposeful and flexible grouping is always a consideration. Visual, auditory, kinesthetic, and tactile approaches may meet the students' preferred learning modalities or support a multisensory approach. Many of the active learning strategies support students at different functioning levels and allow students to contribute their perspective in a number of ways: in written and oral communication, in groups, or individually. Choosing a strategy to support learners well means that teachers have already identified the abilities and profiles of their students and have considered content and presentation. It often means encouraging students to understand multiple viewpoints and share reflections. Each child is different, and the strategies in this book are designed to help educators develop their repertoire of strategies in order to meet specific student needs effectively. Although many of the strategies are movement and cooperation based (such as Ball Toss, Spider Web, and Jigsaw), others are individual and reflective (such as Exit Cards and Information Rings; see Chapter 4). Teachers are invited to adapt and modify strategies to support the differentiated needs of learners.

SUPPORTING STATE STANDARDS AND ASSESSMENTS

At a time when teachers feel overburdened and overpressured by new initiatives, standards, high-stakes assessments, and increased student needs in the classroom, the last thing a teacher needs to do is try yet another idea! However, it can be "Active learning to the rescue!" as opposed to "Please! No more extra work!" Active learning strategies *support* objectives, standards, and assessments rather than *add* to them. Standards-driven instruction can be effectively aligned with differentiation and active learning to create learning experiences that make physical, emotional, and reflective connections to objectives that impact student growth and goal attainment (Gregory & Kuzmich, 2004). Active learning supports the instructional process and product of the classroom by building a community of learners who are cooperative, interactive, and brain compatible. These concepts are aligned with the research that supports standards (Benson, 2009). Standards should support the globalization of learning as teachers are committed to "big ideas" rather than textbook chapters and guides. Lesson choice and design should become clearer with a standards focus (Perna & Davis, 2007).

Although each state has its own academic standards, they typically include goals such as comprehension, writing proficiency, numeric operations and applications, inquiry, analysis, historical perspective, problem solving, comparing, making real-life connections, and so on. Standards set high expectations for students while keeping teachers focused on critical thinking in the learning process. Active learning strategies specifically support standards as well as academic and behavioral objectives. For example, strategies such as Venn Hoops help students compare and contrast concepts. The Paper Pass and Think, Pair, Share can be used to add to, synthesize, and make connections to different concepts (see Chapter 4).

Assessments are designed to measure what students know and what they need to learn in relation to the standards. Grades no longer evaluate what students know. Now educators and politicians are looking at what students know in comparison to others. This does not mean that learning cannot be motivating and meaningful, but it needs to be focused, with deliberate practices to support diverse learners (Benson, 2009; Perna & Davis, 2007). Teachers need to make connections between standards and student achievement, tailoring instruction to provide opportunities to reflect and apply knowledge to real-world contexts. A clear, standards-based curriculum allows for review and application without redundancy, all of which are key components of active learning (Perna & Davis, 2007).

State assessment or high-stakes testing used for promotion, rating, or placement typically brings on undue stress that can be passed from administrator to teacher to student. Families and entire communities can feel anxious and tense until the tests are over. Some teachers feel compelled to teach to the test, and you may hear comments like, "We can finally teach" after assessments are administered. Certainly, state-wide testing is meant to evaluate student performance, *not* to replace instruction, but accountability and competition in the field of education sometimes cause educators to think otherwise. Although assessments, like standards, differ between states and even districts, many of the concepts are the same. Two of the objectives that assessments typically test are

1. Basic skills including reading, writing, and mathematics

2. Subject area content knowledge

Active learning strategies can help teachers meet these two key assessment objectives. They support teachers in their effort to teach, review, and reinforce. For example, basic skills and content knowledge can be reviewed using Ball Toss, Puzzle Pieces, Two Truths and a Lie, Exit Cards, Classroom Box Bingo, Information Rings, and Line Up (see Chapter 4).

The ability to develop concepts to explain and persuade, which writing assessments often require, can be supported by activities such as Barometer, Round Robin, Play Dough Construction, and Walking in Their Shoes (see Chapter 4). Active learning outcomes such as Exit Card information, Paper Pass and Round Robin products, and Job Wanted posters can provide teachers with data on formative and summative objective and standard attainment, thus making student performance evaluations meaningful and generating information to guide future teaching decisions. At the same time, active learning makes dull, difficult, or repetitive material interesting and engaging.

MOTIVATING LEARNERS WITH ACTIVE LEARNING STRATEGIES

Consider the fact that in 1926, John Dewey asked, "Why is it, in spite of the fact that teaching by pouring in, learning by passive absorption, are universally condemned, that they are still so entrenched in practice" (p. 46)? It is hard to believe how history continues to repeat itself.

Motivation refers to students' willingness to engage in lessons and learning activities. For teachers, a major goal of lesson development is to identify motivational strategies that will encourage students to engage in classroom activities that meet specific educational objectives (Brophy, 1997). Engaged students investigate educational content more thoroughly (Zmuda, 2008).

Motivation affects learning. As you read, take a moment to think about your own learning. Recall a situation in which you were highly motivated to learn. Then contrast this experience with a learning situation in which your motivation was low (or maybe nonexistent). What was the difference? Why? How can we use what we know about our own learning experiences to shape our teaching and encourage our students to be active participants in their own learning?

When students report high levels of motivation to learn, four factors are generally present: the opportunity to learn; facilitators who probe for student response; support for student learning through modeling; and scaffolding and evaluation. Strategies that incorporate these factors, such as the strategies in this book, will result in increased student motivation and involvement.

We also acknowledge that increased time, curriculum, and standards constraints have left teachers with little room to devote to process and outcome connections. With the shift in focus from teaching to learning in an era of accountability, it is important to support teachers in their efforts to find motivating strategies that will improve achievement for diverse learners. Uguroglu and Walberg (1979) provide substantial evidence that motivation is consistently and positively related to educational achievement. Research also clearly indicates that active learning engages and motivates diverse students in the learning process *and* has resulted in increased performance outcomes (Carroll & Leander, 2001; Ginsberg, 2005; Rugutt, 2004; Smart & Csapo, 2001; K. Wood, 2008).

Active learning can be an effective and essential instructional component of the inclusive classroom. Students with special needs who are actively involved and engaged tend to learn more and faster. Hands-on interactive learning appeals to the senses and provides a reason to learn, promotes attention to task, and may lessen negative behaviors (Choate, 2004).

The ability to motivate students is fundamental to equity in teaching and learning, and it is a core virtue of educators who successfully differentiate instruction (Tomlinson & Allan, 2000). Awareness of and respect for diversity, such as cultural differences, encourages teachers to invite the experiences, concerns, opinions, and perspectives of diverse students to be shared and valued in the learning process. Lessons that respect diversity are especially motivating for students from low-socioeconomic communities. Students will be more motivated to learn when their voices and perspectives are shared and valued and connections to personal experience are made. Learners will be more engaged by teachers who help them connect to and respect one another in the learning process (Ginsberg, 2005). Overall, teachers can redesign the teaching and learning environment by providing different learning strategies to different students and finding ways to motivate students to learn as they engage them in the active learning process (Rugutt, 2004).

As we will explain in Chapter 2, active learning strategies are not one-size-fits-all. Each strategy shared in this book must be carefully examined to make sure it can be used to make meaningful connections to student needs, interests, and abilities while clearly connecting to lesson objectives and purpose and appropriate state standards. Although some active learning strategies are cooperative and others are individual in nature, all provide distinct alternatives to lecturing and identify the student as the center of the learning process. Encouraging engagement and motivation ultimately enhances learner outcomes for all students.

ACCESS IS NOT ENOUGH: THE CRITICAL NEED TO ADDRESS DIVERSE STUDENT POPULATIONS

The conception of disabilities has changed dramatically in the past several hundred years in a multitude of ways. Historically, people with pronounced disabilities were, more often than not, beggars walking around with cap in hand, looking for money with which to support themselves. Hence, the term *handicapped*, derived from "cap in hand." Today, we try to include and value individuals with disabilities in society and in the education process.

As a result of recent legislation, the critical need to address diverse student populations has become more and more apparent. From 1954 to 1975, landmark legislation tried to protect and include diverse student populations in the educational process. *Brown* v. *Board of Education* (1954) ruled that segregation based on race and other educational factors was unconstitutional. *Hansen* v. *Hobsen* (1967) ruled that ability grouping or tracking violated due process and equal protection under the constitution. In 1970, *Diana* v. *State Board of Education* required that children be tested in their primary language. In 1975, the Education for All Handicapped Children Act (PL 94–142) mandated that students with disabilities must receive the most appropriate services and are entitled to receive a free and appropriate public education in the least restricted environment (LRE; Gable & Hendrickson, 2004). The LRE clause of PL 94–142 and the Regular Education Initiative (REI) from the 1980s called for the restructuring of special and general education, supporting the inclusion of at-risk students, culturally diverse students, and students with disabilities in the general education classroom (Gable & Hendrickson, 2004).

Unfortunately, many years later, students with learning differences were still excluded from the general education curriculum. Schools and teachers were not held accountable for the achievement and performance of students with special needs. In 1997, the Individuals with Disabilities Education Act (IDEA) required inclusion of individuals with disabilities in the general education curriculum, holding the general and special education teachers accountable for the achievement of students classified with special needs (Karten, 2005).

Moreover, in 2001, President George W. Bush introduced the No Child Left Behind Act (NCLB; PL 107–110), which made schools accountable for the performance of many diverse populations, including students with diverse ethnic and cultural backgrounds, students with disabilities, males and females, and students of varying socioeconomic status. Differentiated assessments are selected by specific states and schools, to identify and report the Annual Yearly Progress of the school as well as the disaggregated data from diverse student groups. All student achievement must be recorded in school data, and teachers are expected to implement research-based instructional practices to support quality education for all students. Thus, in an era of inclusion and accountability, access is not enough. Educators are more responsible for quality of instruction and diverse student population performance than ever before.

Legislation and the inclusion movement have not just relocated children from self-contained to inclusive classrooms. The movement has had a serious impact on the roles and responsibilities of teachers. General educators are responsible for the performance of growing numbers of diverse students in their classroom. To ensure the success of students, general and special educators must work collaboratively to combine the knowledge of what to teach with the knowledge of how to teach (Choate, 2004). Educators often appreciate diverse learners in their classrooms but feel they lack the resources and expertise needed to support their learning (Bruneau-Balderrama, 1997; Mastropieri, 2001; Snyder, 1999). Teachers need the skills and experience to meet the specific needs of different students in the classroom so they feel empowered to teach successfully (Cook, 2002; O'Shea, 1999). Rather than dispense knowledge, an educator should guide and facilitate interaction to encourage learners to question and challenge ideas, opinions, and conclusions. Active learning has numerous positive attributes and is independent of age, cross-cultural, easy to acquire, and independent of measures of intelligence (Jensen, 2001).

THE BEGINNING

At the beginning of this chapter, we invited you to take a journey with us. We hope you're ready. Right now, if you choose to come along, you'll need a few things:

- An understanding of your inclusive student population (consider classification, age, interest, learning styles, dynamics, ability, strengths and needs, etc.);
- Curriculum—goals and objectives for specific units and lessons—and state standards that inform the curriculum;
- A careful look at the learning environment in your classroom (consider furniture, floor and wall space, etc.);

- A willingness to adapt and be flexible;
- A willingness to reflect;
- Motivation to excite and engage your students with *your own enthusiasm* for teaching and learning; and
- Sun-tan lotion (Okay, wishful thinking on our part).

CHAPTER 1 SUMMARY

- Inclusion is the term used to describe the education of students with disabilities in the general education classroom with appropriate supports and services to enable them to succeed.
- Teachers need to be equipped with a repertoire of strategies to support diverse learners in the inclusive classroom.
- Active learning is the intentional engagement of students in the learning process, supporting behavioral and cognitive objectives as well as appropriate state standards. Students are engaged and having fun and, at the same time, are the center of their own learning experience.
- Active learning strategies create an instructional design to support brain-based learning because they can help students increase energy levels, make connections to concepts, motivate students to learn, and support long-term memory.
- Legislation such as IDEA and NCLB continues to increase the number of students with classifications in the inclusive classroom, making special and elementary education teachers accountable for diverse student performance.
- Active learning strategies can support attainment of state standards and successful performance on state assessments.
- Active learning can support teachers in their efforts to differentiate instruction to improve performance of classified and nonclassified students. These strategies can support all learners.

2

Selecting and Implementing Active Learning Strategies for the Inclusive Classroom

INTRODUCTION

I remember clearly the first time I was introduced to the Ball Toss strategy. I was at an Open House to meet the teachers in my son's third-grade class. His math teacher, Mrs. M., was a brand-new teacher, enthusiastic and engaging. She explained that if our sons and daughters came home and reported that all they did in math class was play games, we should understand that they were really learning and were, in fact, practicing their math facts. To illustrate her point, she showed us a Nerf football with math facts on it and described how she used it in class. (I do remember wishing that I had teachers who taught that way when I was a student!)

The talk was enlightening to the group assembled, and I am sure that more than one parent felt secure in the knowledge that the new math teacher was really teaching. But Mrs. M.'s message is an important one, and it is perhaps the key to the effective use of strategies. Simply put, the purpose of using strategies is to teach content. We are looking to motivate, to engage, and to involve our students in the learning process, and having students enjoy what they are doing is always a plus, but the bottom line is the teaching and learning.

To that end, it is crucial to know the purpose of the lesson for which you are choosing a strategy and to keep the lesson objective(s) in the forefront when choosing the strategy, planning and implementing the lesson, and developing the assessment.

Equally important is to know your students and how they learn best. This chapter is designed to help you choose, use, and reflect on active learning strategies to maximize learning and understanding in your inclusive classroom.

CLASSIFICATIONS AND CHARACTERISTICS

IDEA is the federal legislation that defines classifications for students with disabilities. These classifications help to identify students who are entitled to special education support and services in public school. Classifications are determined by a team of evaluation experts using a child study multidisciplinary team approach and are accepted by parents before identification and placement. Students with disability classifications will be part of the inclusive classroom.

IDEA classifications for students with disabilities are described in Figure 2.1 (Mastropieri & Scruggs, 2000, pp. 10–11).

Figure 2.1   IDEA Classification Chart

Autism: A developmental disability significantly affecting verbal and nonverbal communication and social interaction, generally evident before age three, that adversely affects educational performance.

Communication Disorder: A disorder of articulation, fluency, voice, or language that adversely affects educational performance, or a severe communication deficit that may require the use of an augmentative or alternative communication system such as sign language, communication boards, or electronic devices.

Deaf-blindness: Individuals in this category have moderate to severe impairments in both vision and hearing. This included as a separate category because of the unique learning needs presented and specialized services required.

Hearing Impairments: Hearing impairments can range from mild to moderate to severe. The hearing loss, with or without amplification, affects educational performance and developmental progress.

Cognitive Impairment (sometimes referred to as mental retardation): Significantly below-average intellectual functioning, with concurrent deficits in adaptive behavior. Individuals with cognitive impairments may exhibit generalized problems in learning, memory, attention, problem solving, and social functioning. It is manifested between birth and age 18 and negatively affects educational performance.

Multiple Disabilities: This category includes any individual with two or more disabling conditions. However, this category often includes cognitive impairment as one of the classifications and is usually used when disorders are serious and interrelated to such an extent that it is difficult to identify the primary area of disability. It does not include deaf-blindness.

(Continued)

Figure 2.1 (Continued)

Orthopedic Impairments: These are associated with physical conditions that seriously impair mobility or motor activity. This category includes individuals with cerebral palsy or diseases of the skeleton or muscles and accident victims.

Other Health Impairments: This category includes chronic or acute health-related difficulties that adversely affect educational performance and is manifested by limited strength, vitality, or alertness. It can include such health problems as heart conditions, sickle cell anemia, and diabetes.

Emotional Disturbance: This category includes individuals with a condition in one or more of the following areas for an extended period of time: (1) an inability to learn not due to intellectual, sensory, or other health problems; (2) inability to build and maintain social relationships with peers and teachers; (3) inappropriate behavior and affect; (4) general pervasive depression and unhappiness; (5) tendency to develop fears or physical symptoms associated with school and personal problems; and (6) schizophrenia.

Specific Learning Disabilities: This refers to a disorder in one or more of the basic psychological processes involved in understanding or using spoken or written language, which can result in difficulties in reading, writing, listening, speaking, thinking, spelling, or mathematics.

Traumatic Brain Injury: This is an acquired injury to the brain due to external force resulting in total or partial functional disability or psychosocial impairment or both, which adversely affects a child's educational program.

Visual Impairments: This is a loss of vision that, even when corrected, affects educational performance. It may be mild to moderate to severe in nature.

OTHER DIVERSE POPULATIONS

Diverse student populations that are found among typically functioning students include culturally and linguistically diverse students, at-risk students, and gifted and talented students. *Culturally and linguistically diverse students* may have customs, traditions, and values that set them apart from their peers and interfere with their self-esteem and their ability to participate in the learning experience. Some may be fluent in English, but others may be English Language Learners. Students who are linguistically diverse may develop communication problems (Lewis & Doorlag, 2006). These students come from all racial, ethnic, and socioeconomic groups. They are most often placed in general education classes; they may need additional help, and they often benefit from the same modifications that are made for children who are classified with higher incidence disabilities (Mastropieri & Scruggs, 2000).

At-risk students are students whose current performance and future welfare are threatened by a host of complex societal issues including poverty; substance, physical, or emotional abuse; and homelessness. These students come to school with additional educational needs and require additional assistance so they don't become part of a school failure statistic (Lewis & Doorlag, 2006). Depending on the nature of the "at-risk" child, some may have "limited experience" learning characteristics.

Gifted and talented students are students who learn more quickly than their peers and are unusually bright. They excel in all academic areas. Some gifted students are more creative and have special talent in art or music. Opportunities for them to express themselves should be provided in the inclusive classroom (Lewis & Doorlag, 2006).

Average learners are general education students who have no classifications for disabilities and are not considered diverse because of culture, language, aptitude, talent, or social problems. These students comprise at least 50% of the inclusive classroom populations. They typically function academically and emotionally at the appropriate age and grade level (Kame'enui, Carnine, Dixon, Simmons, & Coyne, 2002). Although they have no label or classification, certainly average learners are individuals with specific learning characteristics who will benefit from active learning strategies that suit their individual academic, social, and personal needs.

ASSESSING STUDENTS AND IDENTIFYING LEARNING CHARACTERISTICS

It is important for teachers to understand disability classifications and determine which learning characteristics each student possesses. Learning characteristics describe how a child learns and include his or her abilities, needs, dispositions, and preferences, such as learning styles and teaching modalities. Although diverse students are often labeled and described with a variety of terms, they have different individual learning characteristics that will determine how they process and retain information. Some learning characteristics apply to all students, with and without classifications. Students' learning characteristics will influence the choices teachers make to present, reinforce, connect, build, and reflect on the active learning process.

Students with disabilities have individual education plans that identify strengths, needs, and strategies. For all students, teachers may use a number of other assessment tools, such as learning style inventories, multiple intelligence surveys, interest surveys and interviews, observations, anecdotal records, error and task analyses, and so on. The important message is that teachers need to know their students. Teachers often feel overloaded and overwhelmed by teaching constrictions. They are told they need to teach to standards, curriculum, state regulations, district initiatives, and so on, but their priority is to teach to their *students!*

Knowing the students is critical when designing instruction. The strategies provided in Chapter 4 give teachers the freedom to select active learning experiences that meet the needs of the different learners in the inclusive classroom. The focus here is not just on students with disability classifications; the focus is on all students in the class, who they are as learners, and what they bring to the learning process. The questions teachers should ask are (1) How does each of my students learn as individuals? (2) How does the class learn as a group? (2) What does each student bring to the learning process? and (3) What can I provide for the learning process to be successful?

USING STRATEGIES: BEFORE, DURING, AND AFTER

Figure 2.2 is designed to help you to operationalize the active learning process. We imagine the reader saying, "Okay, I am with you so far. Now what?" The charts that follow provide guidance in the following:

- selecting a strategy that is appropriate for the content of a specific lesson;
- selecting a strategy to meet individual student needs;
- guiding the implementation process; and
- reflecting, which includes questions to consider after using the strategy.

Figure 2.2 Before the Strategy

Considerations When Choosing a Strategy

When you are choosing a strategy, ask yourself the following questions:

- What are my specific academic objectives for this lesson?
- How does the strategy address appropriate state standards?
- Is the strategy a good fit with these objectives?
- If there are academic prerequisite skills students need to be successful with this strategy, do my students have the skills at this time?
- Do I have affective/social skill objectives for this lesson (e.g., working in groups)?
- Are there specific affective/social skills that students need in order to be successful with this strategy (e.g., working in groups), and if so, do they have these skills currently?
- What are the strengths and limitations of my diverse learners, and which strategies tend to accentuate those strengths?
- Does this strategy mirror the strengths of the class, as opposed to its weaknesses?
- What physical space do I need for this to work (e.g., the classroom space can be used as is; the classroom can be used if desks are pushed back; the hallway is available; the playground is off limits)?
- What materials do I need, and are they readily available or do I have to collect them and bring them to school? Can I use this strategy today or only after I have brought in the materials I need?
- Is this a strategy I can implement easily, or do I need time to prepare?
- Does this strategy fit with my needs, strengths, and comfort level?

HOW TO CHOOSE A STRATEGY TO MEET INDIVIDUAL STUDENT NEEDS

All the strategies we offer are designed to engage and motivate students and to facilitate and encourage learning. Although these strategies were developed for use with a variety of different learners and have a variety of applications, some strategies do address specific learning needs more directly than others. Consequently, Figure 2.3 indicates the learning characteristics each strategy addresses.

Figure 2.3 Strategies That Address Specific Learner Characteristics

Strategies	Learner Characteristics									
	Metacognitive Issues	Auditory Processing Concerns	Memory Issues	Low Experiential Base	Attention Needs	Higher Aptitude Learners	Interpersonal Preferences	Language Needs	Social Skills Issues	Visual Processing Concerns
Acrostic Topics		*				*	Individual or small group			
Baggie Stories	*	*	*		*		Small group	*		
Ball Toss		*	*		*		Whole group			*
Barometer	*				*	*	Whole group			*
Chain Reaction	*				*		Whole group			*
Classification Capers		*		*	*		Small group	*		*
Classroom Box Bingo			*		*		Whole group		*	*
Exit Cards	*	*	*				Individual	*		
Fishbowl				*			Whole group			*
Four Corners				*	*		Whole group			*
Howdy Partner!			*		*	*	Individual or whole group			*
If I Were . . .	*						Whole group	*	*	*
Information Rings		*	*				Individual or small group	*		

(Continued)

Figure 2.3 (Continued)

Strategies	Learner Characteristics									
	Metacognitive Issues	Auditory Processing Concerns	Memory Issues	Low Experiential Base	Attention Needs	Higher Aptitude Learners	Interpersonal Preferences	Language Needs	Social Skills Issues	Visual Processing Concerns
Job Wanted Poster	*	*				*	Individual or small group			
Line Up!		*			*		Small group	*		
Listening Teams	*	*	*		*	*	Whole group with small group support			*
Outline Plus	*	*	*		*		Individual	*		*
Paper Pass		*	*	*		*	Individual or small group			
People Movers		*	*		*		Whole group or small group	*		
Play Dough Construction				*	*		Individual or small group	*		*
Puzzle Pieces		*	*		*		Whole group or small group	*	*	
Quick Questions	*	*				*	Individual or small group	*		*
Rainbow Ball		*		*	*		Whole group or small group		*	
Round Robin		*			*	*	Small group			
Sentence Starter	*	*	*			*	Whole group or small group		*	
Snowball Fight		*		*	*	*	Whole group		*	

Learner Characteristics

Strategies	Metacognitive Issues	Auditory Processing Concerns	Memory Issues	Low Experiential Base	Attention Needs	Higher Aptitude Learners	Interpersonal Preferences	Language Needs	Social Skills Issues	Visual Processing Concerns
Spider Web			*		*		Whole group		*	*
Think, Pair, Share	*			*	*	*	Pair	*	*	*
Timeline	*		*				Small group			*
Two Truths and a Lie					*		Small group		*	*
Venn Hoops	*	*			*	*	Small group			
Walking in Their Shoes				*		*	Whole group		*	
What's in the Bag?		*		*	*	*	Individual or small group	*		
What Up?					*		Individual	*		*
What Would It Say?		*		*	*		Small group			*
Who Am I? What Am I?	*				*		Whole group or small group			*
52 Things to Do			*	*		*	Whole group or small group	*		*
Conversation Cues					*		Individual		*	
Conversation Cards		*			*	*	Whole group or small group	*	*	*
The Whip		*			*		Whole group		*	*

We have chosen to focus on learning characteristics because they provide information about what makes each of us unique in terms of how we learn. In addition, learning characteristics cut across disability categories. A child can have difficulties focusing because of one or more disabilities, or because he or she is distracted due to home issues, or just because he or she needs some help with staying focused.

LEARNER CHARACTERISTICS DESCRIBED

Metacognitive Issues

Metacognition is defined as "awareness and understanding of one's thinking and cognitive processes; thinking about thinking" (Merriam-Webster Online, 2010). Metacognition "emphasizes self-awareness of how one approaches a task in order to plan and monitor progress" (Sliva, 2004, p. 72). Students who are more proficient at metacognition are more successful at attempting and completing new learning tasks (Sliva, 2004). Strategies that emphasize process and enable the learner to create and explain a concrete plan support these students (e.g., Timeline and Outline Plus).

Metacognition strategies are also used to provide feedback on one's own learning. Examples of such metacognitive strategies are making predictions, checking progress, and monitoring work (Lenz & Deshler, 2004). Think, Pair, Share is a strategy that can achieve these goals. Self-regulation, or adjusting one's own performance, is also a component of metacognition (Hallahan & Kauffman, 2006). A student with a low-incidence disability may have difficulty self-regulating, and so may a student with social immaturity or other needs. Again, strategies that support planning and evaluating will help students monitor their own behavior and organize and process ideas.

Auditory Processing

"Auditory processing refers to an individual's ability to analyze, interpret, and process information obtained through the ear. It does not apply to what is received by the eardrum or to deafness, or being hard of hearing" (Sliva, 2004, p. 19). Students need to be able to interpret and use what they hear.

Children with perceptual-auditory concerns can have problems discriminating sounds. They may have difficulty determining the difference between words with similar sounds, such as *fix* and *fit*. Fine and gross motor skills can be affected when tasks involve motor and visual or verbal skills simultaneously. Strategies that pair auditory and visual stimuli will support learners who have difficulties with auditory processing, (e.g., Information Rings).

Visual Processing

"Students with visual-processing difficulties have trouble making sense of information visually. Some implications of these difficulties include losing their place on a page or worksheet or while reading a text; confusing unrelated information on a page; reversing letters or digits; and the inability to differentiate objects based on their individual characteristics" (Sliva, 2004, p. 28).

For example, children with visual processing issues may have trouble solving puzzles and remembering shapes (Hallahan & Kauffman, 2006). Strategies that use multi-modalities and multisensory approaches, pairing visual stimuli with other modalities, enhance learning for these students. Discussion also supports the learning experience for students with visual processing concerns. Strategies such as What's in the Bag? and Two Truths and a Lie will benefit these students.

Memory Issues

Students with memory deficits typically have difficulty remembering information. Such students may

- understand new information in class but be uncertain how to proceed once they leave class,
- have difficulty placing information in short-term memory and thus have problems later retrieving it from long-term memory,
- not easily retrieve needed information from long-term memory. (Sliva, 2004, p. 20)

As explained in Chapter 1, brain-based information processing research tells us that the way in which new information is stored affects how easily and quickly it can be retrieved when needed (i.e., the "I have it on the tip of my tongue" phenomenon). Therefore, new ideas and information need to be connected to prior knowledge, in order to facilitate information retrieval. An example of a strategy that helps students create connections and build memory is the Paper Pass.

To move information from short-term to long-term memory, students need to rehearse it. Memory skills are necessary for students to retrieve, connect, and apply information. Strategies that include chunking, review, rehearsal, and reinforcement will support learners with memory issues (e.g., Puzzle Pieces and Ball Toss).

Low Experiential Base

Low experiential base refers to children who, for a variety of reasons, have not been exposed to many of the life experiences that most children of the same age or grade level have. They may be culturally diverse or at risk. Vocabulary is likely to be impacted. These children may not be able to relate to a story, for example, not because of lack of ability but because of lack of experience or exposure to key elements or concepts in the story. Student background can limit or enhance comprehension of new material. Strategies that provide exposure to new ideas and vocabulary will support these students (e.g., What's in the Bag?).

Attention Issues

Attention affects how well children are able to maintain their concentration on a topic (Sliva, 2004). Movement and novelty will often interest and motivate students with attention issues (Kounin, 1977). Active learning strategies can engage the learner who has difficulty with attention and hyperactivity by providing movement and kinesthetic activities and presenting information and learning activities in brief intervals (e.g., Round Robin and Spider Web).

Social Skills Issues

Students with poor or limited social skills have difficulty engaging appropriately with their peers. They seem less mature, reticent, or have low self-esteem. They have trouble reading social cues and misinterpret the feelings and emotions of others, often responding inappropriately (Hallahan & Kauffman, 2006; Mastropieri & Scruggs, 2000). They can be ignored and left out or ridiculed by others. They may not understand when they are bothering others, and they may not know how to view things from another person's perspective. Strategies that promote role play or group interaction, turn-taking directions, and peer support (such as Think, Pair, Share) can support individuals with social skills issues.

Higher Aptitude Learners

The higher aptitude learners are the students who need an additional academic challenge. Students who can be described as "gifted and talented" fall under this category. Students with other classifications, such as behavioral issues, can also have high aptitude. They benefit from lessons that include multiple entry points (e.g., Round Robin), such as working with the same content at different levels of Bloom's taxonomy or using a different set of resources (Heacox, 2002).

Interpersonal Preferences

Some children have distinct preferences in terms of who they work with. During the course of the week, some lessons require children to work with the whole group; other lessons focus on small group work, cooperative learning, pairs, or working individually. Keep in mind that some of the active learning strategies can be adapted to meet different interpersonal preferences. For example, the Paper Pass may be an individual or cooperative experience. Spider Web may be used with the whole group. Round Robin can be used to support cooperative learning groups. Two Truths and a Lie supports small group interaction.

Language

There are children who are English Language Learners. There are children who have difficulty with expressive language, which impacts a child's ability to explain things verbally or complete such tasks as rapid oral drills. There are children who have difficulty with receptive language; this type of learner has difficulty connecting vocabulary words to their meaning (Sliva, 2004). Students who have one or more of these language issues may need additional time or prompts to answer questions, practice with vocabulary words, or the opportunity to demonstrate an answer rather than explain it verbally (e.g., Information Rings). Visual or concrete props in a strategy will support extemporaneous speech (e.g., Play Dough Construction).

The Importance of It All

We know that all people have both strengths and weaknesses in terms of how they learn best. If we identify a weakness and avoid it in order to encourage success, we run the risk of weakening this learning modality even further. The idea is to teach to the strengths and remediate the weaknesses. Figure 2.3 suggests which strategies may give children the chance to practice and strengthen specific learning characteristics that may be affecting the way they comprehend new material.

HOW TO CHOOSE A STRATEGY TO MEET INDIVIDUAL TEACHER NEEDS

The purpose of this book is to empower you as the teacher in the classroom. Take into account your own strengths, needs, preferences, and skills when you choose strategies. Although it is important to design lessons to support how children learn, it is also important to consider yourself as well. Who are you as a teacher? What is your comfort level with movement and transition?

Consider your teaching style. How can you best facilitate your class? Would you benefit from trying something new? Be sure you are comfortable with the complexity of the strategy before using it. Practice strategy implementation before introducing it to the class. Although we recommend new ideas, teacher motivation and enthusiasm will certainly impact the success of the student learning experience. Figures 2.4 through 2.6 (see pages 27–29) will help you consider which strategies may be most useful for you and your class and determine whether the strategies were successful.

LEARNING COMMUNITIES

In many schools, teachers are forming learning communities to continue to study teaching and learning. The questions posed in this chapter lend themselves to discussion, whether you have established a formal learning community with set hours and agenda or have more informal discussions with the fourth-grade teachers, the child study team members you work with, or the people you eat lunch and share your successes and frustrations with. Often in inclusive classrooms, two teachers are working together to maximize learning. The questions in Figure 2.6 are designed to open a meaningful dialogue on planning for instruction in any and all of these situations.

AND NOW, THE NEXT STEP ON OUR JOURNEY

We have worked our way through the reason why active learning is so important (Chapter 1) and the nitty gritty on how to choose and apply the strategies (Chapter 2). Stick with us as we discuss why and how to use grouping for instruction in the inclusive classroom (Chapter 3) and then describe the strategies (Chapter 4).

CHAPTER 2 SUMMARY

- Students who receive special education services must have one of the IDEA classifications: autism, communication disorder, deaf-blindness, hearing impairment, cognitive impairment, multiple disabilities, orthopedic impairments, other health impairment, emotional disturbance, traumatic brain injury, or visual impairment.
- Diverse groups among typically functioning students include culturally and linguistically diverse students, at-risk students, average learners, and the gifted and talented.
- All these students, with and without classification, can benefit from active learning strategies in the inclusive classroom. In order to identify which strategies will support specific learners, look at the students' individual learning characteristics. A description of each of these characteristics and the type of strategies that will support these needs are included in the chapter. Learner characteristics include metacognitive issues, auditory processing concerns, memory issues, low experiential base, attention needs, higher aptitude learners, language needs, social skills deficits, and visual processing concerns.
- Figure 2.3 identifies the 40 active learning strategies and their corresponding learner characteristics.
- Figures 2.2 and 2.4 through 2.6 help the teacher consider strategy selection and implementation for specific student needs and then reflect on the lesson.

Figure 2.4   During the Strategy

Considerations for Implementing a Strategy

- Make a direct connection between the activity and what you want students to learn.

- Establish the purpose of the lesson so that students know what the objectives are and what they will be learning (e.g., "We are going to practice multiplication facts" or "During today's lesson, I want you to gather facts that you can use in the essay on . . . that each student will write tomorrow"). This is particularly helpful for children with specific learning disabilities, to help them to relate new content to previously learned material in order to enhance the short-term and long-term memory storage and retrieval.

- Consider your process and outcome for the lesson.

- Gather and/or construct materials and try them out before the lesson so you know they will work the way they are supposed to (e.g., Does the marker work on the material that you need to write on?).

- Use your closure to assess what the students learned and reflect on the experience. What are you expecting your students to learn? During closure, what have the students produced, connected, reflected on, or concluded?

Figure 2.5 After the Strategy

Considerations After Using a Strategy

- Did the students learn what I wanted them to learn?

- How do I know that the students learned what I wanted them to learn?

- Were the students able to follow the directions? Should I modify the way I give directions or how I explain what they need to do?

- Were all students motivated and engaged? Did everyone appear to be comfortable participating?

- Did this strategy enhance the experience of classroom community and allow diverse learners to work together productively?

- What would I do differently next time?

- Could I bring in more comparisons or develop more syntheses, such as alternative perspectives and text-to-text or text-to-self connections?

- What other academic content can I use with this strategy?

- What were the benefits of using this strategy (e.g., It spurred a lively conversation about the content)?

- Were there any drawbacks to this strategy (e.g., It took more time than expected)?

- Would I recommend it to my colleagues? Why or why not?

- Will I consider using it again?

- Rate your own enthusiasm/motivation for this strategy.

Figure 2.6 Reflections

Teacher Notes and Reflections

My thoughts

_____

_____

_____

How this connects to my philosophy of inclusion

_____

_____

_____

What I want to share with colleagues

_____

_____

_____

Connections to my students' learning characteristics

_____

_____

_____

When I consider my students this year, what learning needs do I feel take precedence as I plan for instruction?

_____

_____

_____

My "aha!" moments

_____

_____

_____

My questions

_____

_____

_____

3

Grouping for Instruction

Who Goes Where With Whom to Do What?

INTRODUCTION

A young couple we know had a private wedding ceremony and then planned a destination weekend celebration to include friends and extended family. The celebration, which was held at a rustic resort, was designed so that the families of the bride and groom could get to know each other. To that end, at the Saturday night dinner, half the people seated at each table were from the bride's family and half from the groom's family.

In order to facilitate conversation, the couple made up a family crossword puzzle and left one copy on each table, along with several pencils. Half the clues focused on the bride's family, and the other half were about the groom's family. Soon enough, puzzles were being solved and conversation flowed.

Incidentally, the bride and groom are both educators. They understood that simply putting people who do not know each other together may not be enough; instead, they created a task that required input and expertise from both sides (in this case, the two families).

The implications for the inclusive classroom are clear. Putting diverse learners in the general education classroom is certainly the first step, but only the first step. The goal is to develop a true classroom community, where students work together, accept one another, and everyone is truly included. Flexible grouping, with attention to how and why children are grouped, is the first step in developing a classroom community.

HOW DO I MANAGE EVERYONE?

A frequent concern about the inclusion classroom is how to meet everyone's learning needs. Parents worry that the content will be taught too slowly, and consequently, significant areas of the curriculum will be inadequately covered. They think perhaps that some children may be bored. Teachers ask how they can meet a variety of needs at one time. Some envision the educational equivalent of the three-ring circus, where everyone needs something different, all at the same time, and a ringmaster is needed to keep some sort of order.

Philosophically, the inclusion classroom is designed so that children learn together. The challenge is to meet individual learning needs in a way that keeps the group cohesive. There are two key issues here. The first is that when teachers use sound educational practices, including active learning strategies, the whole class benefits.

The purpose of active learning strategies is to teach, reinforce, and practice content. One of the benefits is that the strategies we discuss in this book accommodate a variety of different learning needs at one time. The strategies that are so important for children with specialized learning needs are, in fact, effective for nonclassified students as well. As we often tell our preservice teachers, "Good teaching is good teaching."

The second key is flexible grouping. When grouping is flexible, children do not have to work with the same group members every lesson, every day, every week. Is it really an inclusive classroom if you group all the classified children together for every single lesson all day long? Flexible grouping enables children to work with, and get to know, a variety of classmates over the course of the year. "Students with special needs benefit from both whole group (or large group) and small group instruction" (Friend & Bursuck, 2009, p. 169).

Flexible grouping is an important component of inclusion and of any instruction that is differentiated, but groups should not isolate a particular population. Flexible grouping, which includes whole group instruction, small group instruction, pairs, and children working individually, creates a wide range of options. Teachers can decide which type of group to use, depending on the active learning strategy, lesson content, and learning needs.

Many of the active learning strategies in this book are designed to be used with the whole group. "The challenge in a whole-group setting of diverse learners is to avoid teaching solely in the way you were taught or the way you learn best" (Hollas, 2007, p. 16). We need to use a variety of strategies in an inclusive classroom in order to reach many different learners.

WHOLE GROUP INSTRUCTION

Sometimes whole group instruction is your most effective teaching method. For example, you'll want to instruct the whole class when you're

- building community through common activities or experiences.
- introducing new units, topics, skills, or concepts.
- conducting discussions of important content. (Heacox, 2002, p. 88)

Building a classroom community is essential for an inclusive classroom. All the children need to be real members of this community, not just physically taking up space in the same room. Active learning addresses this issue. In the first place, when children work together as a class, trying something different, they have the opportunity to relate to one another in a variety of different ways. The strategies change the classroom dynamic so that the fact that a child struggles with reading is not the only thing, or even the first thing, that others notice about him. For example, these strategies allow different strengths and skills to emerge, so a child who struggles academically may be able to show abilities in other areas. (His classmates can see him as the student who can draw really well, as opposed to the one who stumbles when he reads aloud.) Also, many of the strategies in this book have adaptations that focus specifically on community building, which provides opportunities for students to get to know one another as individuals rather than stereotypes.

Some of the strategies we describe involve a physical component; the children have to stand, move, and maybe even catch a ball. Others involve something novel, like throwing a ball of yarn while sharing opinions. In these situations, you can work with the whole group to introduce or expand on new material, but at the same time, take into consideration individual learning needs. These strategies can, for example, give children the chance to move in a purposeful way to help them to focus on what they are learning. For example, it is more beneficial for the child with ADHD to engage in purposeful movement than to sit at a desk writing for a solid hour. Structured movement can help the student to focus on the task at hand.

Class discussions, as noted, are important. As we discussed in Chapter 2, our active learning strategies that facilitate meaningful discussion among classmates easily accommodate the child who has an expressive language difficulty, for example, depending on how the strategy is implemented. These strategies may be adapted to give a child additional processing time after hearing the question or sentence starter, allow children to speak without having to raise their hands and volunteer, or allow the teacher to engineer whether a given child speaks at the beginning or closer to the end of children's responses.

SMALL GROUP INSTRUCTION

In an inclusive classroom, the teacher can create a variety of groups in the course of a week, depending on the purpose of the lesson and the needs of the children. This enables children to work with different people and get to know all their classmates. It also eliminates the stigma of placing children in the "yellow" group or the "blue" group for everything they do. (Has anyone else heard the story of the teacher who used group names rather than numbers so that children would not know the levels of the groups and then called one group the "roses" and the other the "thorns"? I am thinking this one is just urban legend, but you get the idea.)

Grouping by ability level (which does have a purpose) becomes only one type of group in which children participate; during some subjects or lessons, they may be paired with other lower level readers, and in other lessons, there is a mix of high and low level readers. In still other lessons, the children who prefer basketball are working together. This keeps the spirit of inclusion strong.

There are times when smaller groups are more effective. Some of the strategies we offer are designed for small group work (see Figure 2.3 in Chapter 2). Academic content to be covered will influence which type of group you use for a particular learning experience.

DIFFERENT WAYS TO FORM GROUPS

As we have discussed, flexible grouping is one of the elements in a successful inclusive classroom. The strategies in Chapter 4 utilize a variety of group formats. Some

SAME ABILITY GROUPS

This is grouping by ability level, otherwise know as homogeneous grouping.

What It Looks Like

- Group by reading or math ability.

Benefits

- It can be used to introduce and practice a specific skill when some children need more instruction and practice.
- It is particularly useful when working on content that is sequential (e.g., children have to learn fractions before they can multiply and divide them).
- It gives everyone the chance to feel competent; children with higher ability in a given area can challenge each other, and children with lower ability in this area can work together at the appropriate level and not always have to be the one who needs help.

MIXED ABILITY GROUPS

These are heterogeneous groups.

What It Looks Like

- Groups are organized so that each group is fairly similar to all other groups in terms of ability level, perhaps with one advanced reader, one average reader, and one lower level reader in each group. Or, one child who is good at art or who has more advanced note-taking skills is placed in each group.

(Continued)

(Continued)

Benefits

- Children have a chance to discuss with and learn from a wider range of their classmates.
- Children learn from each other's strengths.
- This promotes classroom community and acceptance of others.
- Students have a variety of role models.

GROUPING BY INTEREST

Groups are formed by grouping students who choose the same topic or subject matter to work on.

What It Looks Like

- Students choose whether they are most interested in studying rural, suburban, or urban lifestyles, or they choose which of five different novels they would like to read.

Benefits

- Children have the opportunity to share common interests.
- This is one way to encourage friendship, tolerance, and understanding of others, and perhaps a mutual appreciation (or dislike) of a new TV show or a sports team will lead to continuing the discussion on the playground or in the lunchroom (one of the goals, and benefits, of inclusion).

GROUPING BY PREFERENCE/LEARNING STYLE

Students identify their favorite learning styles and the teacher uses this information to form groups.

What It Looks Like

- In a project on Greece, several groups have been set up: drawing a mural of Athens, putting on a play about the history of the country, making a travel brochure, compiling and describing several reliable websites about the country, and designing a scrapbook about the country. Children choose which group they want to work with, based on their learning style preference.

Benefits

- It motivates students.
- It capitalizes on, and emphasizes, children's strengths rather than their weaknesses.
- It gives each child the chance to shine.
- It is yet another way to build a classroom community.

STUDENT CHOICE

Children select whom they want to work with.

What It Looks Like

- Children are told to form groups of three.

Benefits

- Children like to choose whom they work with.
- It is effective when it is only one of several methods of grouping.

RANDOM GROUPING

Student groups are formed with no particular plan as to who goes in which group.

What It Looks Like

- Students count off, and all the ones work together, all the twos, and so on, or each child is given a colored paper clip and asked to join the other children with the same color paper clip.

Benefits

- It is efficient and convenient.
- Students have the chance to work with everyone in the class over the course of the school year.

APPARENTLY RANDOM GROUPING

The teacher uses a grouping system that appears to the students to be random, but actually it is not.

What It Looks Like

- Color partners: The teacher does a quick survey of the room and asks all children wearing anything red to get in one corner, all those wearing something yellow to get in another corner, and so on; once a child joins a group, he or she stays there even if wearing an additional color that is called subsequently.
- Clock partners: Each child has a template of a clock in which there is one blank line next to each number; children have to fill in each line with the name of one classmate. If Lydia writes Sam's name next to number 12 on her clock, then she writes her name next to number 12 on Sam's clock. Each name should only be written down once on each sheet, and children should be encouraged to seek out others they do not know well. These students become "clock partners" for

(Continued)

(Continued)

the year; for example, when the teacher wants the class to pair up for a reading assignment, she asks them to sit with their "two o'clock" partners (Michigan Literacy Progress Profile, 2003).

- Shape partners: A simpler version of clock partners in which each child is given a sheet of paper with a different shape in each corner. Students have to write one child's name next to each shape to create shape partners; for example, everyone is asked to meet up with their "triangle" partner for the next lesson (ProTeacher Community, 2006).

Benefits

- It can be done on the spur of the moment once the partner sheets have been completed. Partner sheets can be completed within the first few weeks of school and glued into the cover of a folder or notebook or laminated for durability.
- It may take less time and be more inclusive than asking the students to find someone to pair up with.
- The teacher can control who is working with whom (or which pairs need to be split up) in a subtle way. Children who are at the same reading level may be paired for a particular assignment, for example, or the two most talkative individuals in the room can be separated for a project that requires intense concentration.
- Students have the chance to work with a variety of children throughout the course of the year.

strategies lend themselves better to one particular type of group, while a number of strategies provide the teacher with a choice.

In the remainder of this chapter, we have provided a quick reference guide to group formats: We describe each type of group, what it looks like, and its benefits. We invite you to compare each type of group and revisit this chapter as needed, depending on lesson content, objectives, and individual student learning needs.

Content, student characteristics, academic and behavioral needs, and lesson objectives will determine which type of grouping will be most effective for a specific class's instructional needs at any given time. Varying the way children are

TIPS FOR CHOOSING AND USING INSTRUCTIONAL GROUPS IN INCLUSIVE CLASSROOMS

One of the overarching concerns is building a classroom community; forming, changing, and rearranging groups influence social, affective, and academic outcomes.

- Teach the children "Ask three, then ask me," and post this saying in your classroom.
- At the beginning of the year, teach and practice effective group work, preferably starting with a few assignments in which the content is relatively easy, so the focus can be on how the group works together.
- Remind children that effective groups

> o listen to each member,
> o take turns, and
> o give positive feedback.
> - Post the list of reminders from the previous bullet point in the classroom so students (and the teacher) can refer to it. Have the class practice the reminders as needed.
> - Practice effective feedback. Start by having a compliment circle in which each child has to compliment the student to his or her right.
> - Capitalize on opportunities for groups to process and share what they have learned or produced with the whole class.

grouped maximizes learning opportunities, helps the teacher to effectively manage children with a variety of learning needs, and keeps the classroom inclusive. We have discussed the importance of flexible grouping and described a number of ways to achieve this goal. The tips box contains suggestions to make the process run more smoothly.

AND NOW (DRUM ROLL, PLEASE) . . . THE STRATEGIES

We've discussed the *what*: inclusion and active learning. We've discussed the *why*: Teachers are responsible for addressing diverse student needs in the inclusive classroom. Now we come to the *especially how* part. Many of you may be saying, "Sure, I agree with all that, but the tough job is making it happen." We've been there and know the feeling, but we hope to alleviate that stress with the following chapter. Chapter 4 describes many strategies and how to adapt them to meet the specific needs of your inclusive classroom.

Enjoy, and we hope your students do, too!

CHAPTER 3 SUMMARY

- Flexible grouping can be instrumental to the successful implementation of active learning strategies.
- With the focus on "including" students in active learning, several grouping options are discussed.
- Whole group instruction is often beneficial for community building, introducing new units and ideas, and discussing important concepts.
- Small group instruction can be arranged by like ability, mixed ability, interest, learning styles and preferences, or randomly. The benefits of each are discussed.
- Tips to support appropriate group instruction and management: Change groups to meet different needs, encourage children to help each other before seeking teacher support, encourage students to be patient and positive with one another, and allow time for groups to share outcomes and meaningful feedback with each other.

4

Active Learning Strategies

INTRODUCTION

In Chapter 1, we explained the relevance of active learning and the way in which strategies incorporate active learning and engage the learner. We reviewed the significant role that motivation plays in student learning, and we made a case for increasing motivation to encourage learning and understanding.

In this chapter, we present a wide variety of strategies that promote active learning. These strategies are motivating because they include movement; or interaction with peers; or topics of particular interest; or different ways of rehearsing content; or allow for student voice, divergent answers, or multiple methods of response. They are motivating because they are appealing to students and they are fun.

Each strategy provides a framework for the teacher to develop a variety of lessons that encourage and engage students; teach, reinforce, and facilitate application of content; and provide opportunities for reflection. Our strategies are presented in alphabetical order, with information about how and why to use each strategy. We offer strategies with multiple suggestions for use, and we encourage you to use them as you see fit to benefit your learners while addressing their needs and making connections to the curricula.

STRATEGY 1

Acrostic Topics

Explanation

In small groups, students use the letters from a specific concept to share information about a topic they are learning. This strategy helps students to develop and relate information to a topic by creating a variation of the acrostic poem.

Materials

- Paper and pencils

or

- Poster and markers

Directions

1. Choose a concept from a specific topic you are teaching. Any words related to a concept may be selected for the acrostic activity (e.g., Civil War, matter, recycling).

2. Provide students with handouts that have the words written vertically down the side of the paper or poster, one letter on each line.

3. Instruct students to write an acrostic poem about the concept word, making sure that each line begins with the letter that corresponds to that line.

4. Have students share their responses with each other, or display their work around the room for reinforcement and review.

Sample Applications

Language Arts/Literacy

○ Use the name of a story or novel, a character, or a concept such as metaphor.

Social Studies

○ Use the name of a war, president, historical site, or event.

Science

○ Use any topic related to a unit of study, such as matter and energy, water cycle, rocks and minerals.

Implementation Considerations

Design

- Decide whether you want to choose words for the acrostic topic or allow students to choose their own words to use or to pass on to another group.

- You can choose topics students have already studied, so that the strategy supports review and reinforcement, or you may choose a new topic and allow students to use resources to construct new knowledge. In that case, the activity acts as the introduction to a new unit of study.

Timing

- Some students may finish early, so have another acrostic challenge prepared for them.

How This Strategy Can Support Individuals With Learning Differences

- Teachers may use multiple words of varying difficulty, to provide challenges suited to students with lower and higher abilities.
- Cooperative learning can support concept development through sharing and discussion.
- Classroom resources (e.g., texts, reference books, websites) can be used to develop information about a topic.
- Completed acrostics provide a concise visual summary of the topic.

Sample Acrostic

COLONIES

Came to America for religious freedom

On long trips in boats

Loyalists agreed with the British King

Often people farmed and hunted

No taxation without representation

If you wanted independence you were a patriot

Even kids helped out with chores like cooking or fishing

Some took the Native Americans' land

Vignette Sample (Fourth-Grade Social Studies)

As part of a review of the Colonial Unit, Ms. V. decided to use the Acrostic Topics strategy. She separated the class into five groups of five. She distributed a large sheet of paper with the word COLONIES written horizontally across the top and vertically down the left side of it. Each group had to write an acrostic poem together. After a lively discussion among groups, Ms. V. gave a two-minute warning and then called, "Pencils down!"

She asked students to share their poems with the class, one letter at a time. For the letter C, one group wrote, "Came to America for religious reasons"; another wrote, "Could've died on the way over"; and another wrote the definition "Colonies—13 regions that formed the first states in America." As each letter was called, Ms. V. asked that a new group member share. Students were eager to hear what the others had to say, and gasps of "Oh, man!" and "Good one!" could be heard. Only two groups had a response for the letter E, so Ms. V. told the remaining groups to use their texts or other classroom resources for support. Once they could look at notes and texts, they came up with answers like "Everyone in the family worked," and "Exploration west made new settlements."

After all the groups finished sharing, Ms. V. summarized the lesson by asking the class for the most important things they learned in the unit on colonies. They could choose information from the text or their acrostic poems to respond. The students talked about the difficult life, freedom, and the beginning of a free country. Students were told that during the remaining 10 minutes of the class, they could use their crayons to make illustrations and decorate their acrostic papers. When the bell rang, each group handed in their paper, and Ms. V. put them on a bulletin board around the word Colonies.

STRATEGY 2

Baggie Stories

Explanation

After reading an assignment, students work in small groups to write up and illustrate a portion of what they read on a Ziploc plastic baggie. Groups present their work, in sequential order, and as they present, each baggie panel is zipped to the previous one and displayed on the overhead. The competed visual tells the story and can be displayed in the classroom.

Materials

- Ziploc plastic baggies, sandwich or quart sized (one for each group plus extras as needed)
- Fine-tipped magic markers in a variety of colors (must be permanent markers)
- One pair of scissors
- Overhead projector

Advance Preparation

1. Use one Ziploc plastic baggie for each cooperative group in the classroom.

2. Cut each baggie down both sides and open it out flat. Hold it vertically, with the shortest side at the top.

3. Zip the baggies together to see which side the writing should be on once all the baggies are completed. Place a mark at the top of each baggie on the side that the students will need to write on.

4. Separate the baggies for the students to use.

Source: The directions for how to make and use baggie stories come from *Differentiated Instructional Strategies for Reading in the Content Areas* by Carolyn Chapman and Rita King, Corwin, 2003. We have adapted their idea and elaborated on it.

Directions

1. Pass out one baggie per cooperative group, and be sure to show each group exactly where to position the flattened baggie as they get ready to write on it. This is important because the baggies will be zipped together, and the writing must be in the same direction on all the baggies so it can be read easily.

2. Assign each group a different part of the content to focus on, such as a fact, passage, or step in the assignment.

3. Give students time to read the assignment, or have them listen and observe as you read a story or demonstrate a science experiment.

4. When students have finished reading or listening to you, direct each group to draw a picture on the top half of their baggie and write a caption on the bottom half that illustrates the section of the material they were assigned to focus on. Model this for younger grades.

5. Give the groups time to discuss what is most important in their section of the material and how they should illustrate it.

6. Gather the baggies and zip them together in sequential order. Make sure the writing and pictures are facing the same direction so that the chain of baggie pictures tells a story in logical order. Place the baggie chain on an overhead projector.

7. Ask group to go to the overhead and present their bag as it rolls across the overhead. This gives students a very concrete sense of how all the material fits together.

8. When the lesson is over, tape colored construction paper behind the plastic baggie chain and hang it up in the classroom. This will serve as a visual reinforcement of lesson content.

Sample Applications

Social Studies

- o Study a timeline.
- o Reconstruct the sequence of a historical event.

Science experiment

- o Group 1 writes up and illustrates the list of materials.
- o Group 2 writes up and illustrates the prediction.
- o Group 3 writes up and illustrates the observation.
- o Group 4 writes up and illustrates the results.
- o Group 5 writes up and illustrates what they learned from the experiment and how this information can be applied in the future.
- o When each groups presents, in sequential order, the class hears a compete recap of the science experiment.

Science: Study of the rain forest

- o Each group writes about and illustrates a different layer of the rain forest.
- o As each group reports, they zip their baggie to the previous group's.

Reading

- o Each group writes and illustrates a different part of the story, to recall the entire sequence.

Community Building: Rules

- o At the beginning of the school year, when younger grades are learning a list of classroom rules, baggie stories can be used to reinforce the rules.
- o Each group writes and illustrates a different rule.
- o Completed baggies are zipped together and hung in the classroom (with colored paper taped underneath) as a novel reminder.

Implementation Considerations

This can easily take up a full class period. For shorter periods of time, or shorter attention spans, the strategy can be divided into two or three sections.

- Section 1: Students can be exposed to the content (reading or listening to the story, watching the science experiment demonstration, etc.). Groups should be told ahead of time what their focus will be so they can take notes.
- Section 2: Group members work together to discuss the material and create their baggie.
- Section 3: The groups present their baggies. The completed baggie story makes a great motivator to start the lesson the next day. Students can take turns explaining each panel.

How This Strategy Can Support Individuals With Learning Differences

- The novelty of the baggie and the materials used can increase both interest in and attention to the task at hand.
- It appeals to visual, kinesthetic, and tactile learners.
- It accommodates a variety of strengths. For example, the child who is a good artist, or who is good at explaining information in front of the class, but may struggle in other areas, has a chance to shine.
- When each group presents a baggie, the content of the lesson is broken down into clear, sequential steps, complete with an illustration.
- As each baggie is zipped to the previous one, there is an oral explanation. This is coupled with the visual representation of literally "zipping" Part 1 to Part 2 to Part 3, a very concrete way of illustrating the connection between the events. This has the benefit of pairing auditory and visual stimuli and connecting parts to the whole.

Vignette Sample (Third-Grade Reading)

Mrs. J's class has finished reading Charlotte's Web, *and she wants to review the novel. She assembles the students into eight groups of three people each and gives each group a plastic baggie that is already prepped for the students to write on. She explains that each group will be assigned one section of the story, and their job will be to write about the section on the bottom half of their baggie and to illustrate it on the top half.*

Mrs. J. gives her class the following assignments:

Group 1: Beginning of the book (The sow gives birth to a litter of piglets and Fern begs her father to let the runt live.)

Group 2: Fern is given the pig and names him Wilbur.

Group 3: Wilbur goes to live with Fern's uncle.

Group 4: Wilbur meets Charlotte, the spider.

Group 5: Wilbur becomes a member of the community of animals who live in the cellar of Zuckerman's barn.

Group 6: Charlotte writes words in her web to save Wilbur.

Group 7: Charlotte and Wilbur go to the county fair.

Group 8: Charlotte dies but her eggs hatch, and Wilbur has three of the offspring as his new friends.

Mrs. J. tells the group that they can use the book to refresh their memories and can use the Internet to research picture ideas. She gives them time to discuss the key points in their section of the novel and then to write and illustrate their baggies. Group discussions are animated, and Mrs. J. notices that students seem to stay on task. When everyone is finished, Mrs. J. has Group 1 zip their baggie to Group 2's baggie. Then Group 2 zips their baggie to Group 3's, and so on until all eight groups have zipped their baggies together.

Mrs. J sets up the overhead projector and calls on Group 1 to start. They go to the front of the class and place their section of the long baggie train under the projector while they explain the beginning of the novel to their peers. Then Group 2 goes up, slides the baggie so that their picture and writing show under the projector, and they discuss their section of the novel. This continues until all the groups have a chance to share their illustrations and discuss their sections of the novel.

Related Information and Resources

Chapman and King (2003) have developed 12 examples of response books that teachers can use to differentiate instruction in the classroom. The authors explain that response books can be used "for content assignments for reviews using different formats of book design and shapes, textures of paper, writing fonts, and implements" (p. 79). We feel that response books are particularly well-suited to the inclusive classroom. We have borrowed one of their examples, baggie stories, and have used it as a strategy.

STRATEGY 3

Ball Toss

Explanation

This strategy uses a ball with a variety of questions written on it as a tool for students to discuss, review, and share information and perspectives.

Materials

- Permanent marker
- Ball (e.g., beach ball or Nerf ball)

Advance Preparation

1. Develop a list of questions. Most questions should be related to content, with some humorous or personal interest questions disbursed throughout.

2. Use a marker to write questions all over the ball.

3. Once a question is written, draw a ring around it.

Directions

1. Toss the ball to a student to begin the game. That student answers the question that her left thumb has landed on. If the question has already been asked, the student chooses a question under another finger.

2. If a student has answered a question incorrectly, peers may help out.

3. The ball can only be thrown to those who have not had a turn.

4. Continue tossing the ball until everyone has had a chance or until all questions have been answered.

Sample Applications

Language Arts/Literacy

- o Ask comprehension questions.
- o Write the names of parts of speech (noun, adjective, etc.) and have students provide an example.

Math

- o Math facts (addition, multiplication, etc.)
- o Write numbers on the ball and have students give at least two factors of the number they land on.
- o Write math symbols on the ball (e.g., < and >) and have students explain their meaning.

Social Studies

- o Ask questions about the cause and effect of the Revolutionary War.
- o Ask for definitions of vocabulary related to geographic land forms.
- o Names of famous events or people are written on the ball, and students have to share one related concept.

Science

- o Describe one way a person may help support environmental sustainability.
- o The names of the five senses are written on the ball. Students share examples of the sense on which their thumb lands.

Study Skills

- o Students create possible test questions and answers. Questions and answers are submitted to the teacher, and the teacher writes the students' questions on the ball.

Implementation Considerations

Timing

- Suggested duration no more than 20 to 25 minutes.

Design

- Although all the questions may be academic, including questions with personal interest or humor always creates a sense of fun and community in the class (e.g., What is your favorite movie? Who was your favorite teacher and why?).
- You may have students answer questions related to content even if someone else has already had the same question, to provide additional reinforcement and review.

Tips

- Beach balls are good for ball tosses because they are inexpensive and can be deflated and saved for the future.
- Sometimes even when you use permanent marker, the ink fades after a while, so be sure to save your questions if you plan to use the same ones again.
- Nerf balls would also be effective for math problems, initial or final consonants, or single word or very short questions.

Variation: Cooperative Learning

1. Pair the ball players and let them work cooperatively on one question.

2. Give students an opportunity to respond to or "pass" the question.

3. You can also create more than one ball with the same questions and set up groups to play independently, so more students have an opportunity to respond. If more than one group is using the ball, a key of questions and answers may be distributed to one member who leads the toss.

4. Cooperative teams may have their own balls with different questions posted on each ball. One possibility is to have a Ball A with multiplication facts up to 5 and Ball B with multiplication facts through 12. Each team can practice multiplication facts at their own level.

How This Strategy Can Support Individuals With Learning Differences

- This strategy can support reinforcement and memory with repetition of questions and answers.
- Students with visual processing needs are supported with an auditory learning experience.

Vignette Sample (Fifth-Grade Social Studies)

After learning about the Civil War, students used a ball toss to share and reinforce knowledge and perspectives about this historical event. Questions on the ball included review and reinforcement, student voice, and connections to real life:

- *Tell us about two causes of the Civil War.*
- *Why was Ulysses S. Grant an important leader of the Civil War?*

- *Tell us about your favorite thing to do.*
- *How did the Civil War end?*
- *Like the abolitionists, is there someone or some group today who works to support and protect people? Explain.*
- *In the Patricia Polacco book* Pink and Say, *two boys from different races learn about each other. When have you shared experiences or learned about people from another race or culture?*
- *Why was Harriet Tubman a heroine? Who is one of your personal heroes?*
- *Why was the Battle of Gettysburg important?*
- *Wild card: Tell us anything you have learned about the Civil War.*
- *Tell us about a time you had a conflict with a family member or friend and how it was resolved.*

To prepare for this ball toss, the teacher created student pairs. Students were paired with an individual who was different from them in academic, social, or cultural orientation. Students stood in a circle around the room. Each student got the opportunity to throw the ball. If students wanted, they could confer with their partner before responding. This allowed students to have support from a class peer if needed, but it provided the opportunity for all individuals to contribute to the discussion. If a pair was stumped, they could ask for help from another pair. If the question had already been asked, students could give the answer again. This provided reinforcement or more opportunities to hear the perspectives of others. At other times, students chose to find a question that had not yet been answered.

Overall, the lesson made clear connections to content, synthesis, and real life meaningful experiences of students. Personal questions helped students share individuality and often made the class chuckle. All 24 students had an opportunity to participate at least once during the 45-minute period. Sometimes the teacher asked pairs to comment on the response of their peers, expanding the discussion on the war or personal details.

As the class gathered to move to their next class in another room, a very shy and reticent student commented to the teacher, "Why can't you bring a ball every day?" The class paid attention during the entire activity. They were excited to see who was going to get a personal or historical question. At the end of the 45 minutes, the students started to get a little tired. The teacher considered taking a sitting or walking break in the middle of the ball toss experience. The students were excited to see some of the same questions on the test at the end of the week.

STRATEGY 4

Barometer

Explanation

Barometer incorporates some of the same elements as a debate. The purpose of this strategy is for students to take a stand on a controversial issue the class has been studying, or a situation that has many sides, and to list the reasons that support their opinion. This encourages students to support their opinions with facts and, at the same time, to consider other points of view. A lively discussion often follows.

Materials

- A large classroom with room to spread out (if this is not possible, just rearrange where the groups are seated)
- Paper and pencils for students to take notes

Directions

1. Choose a controversial topic that the students have been studying, one that has many sides to the same issue. Alternatively, propose a situation or a scenario, and see whether students agree or disagree with the process or the outcome. Describe one situation, or ask one open-ended question, for the class to work on for the period.

2. Review the content, and ask students to consider how they feel about this particular issue or situation.

3. Ask students to take a stand on the issue and choose one of the following options:
   o strongly agree—Group 1
   o agree (or tend to agree)—Group 2
   o neutral (do not have a firm opinion one way or the other)—Group 3
   o disagree (or tend to disagree)—Group 4
   o strongly disagree—Group 5

4. Ask students to move into the group that corresponds with the opinion they hold. Groups will discuss why they hold the beliefs they do and list reasons to support their opinion.

5. If room allows, seat the groups in circles along a vertical or diagonal line in the classroom, with Group 1 at the head of the line, then Group 2, and so on, in sequential order.

6. Once groups have had the chance to talk among themselves, give each group five minutes to explain its position to the rest of the class and try to change the opinion of the other groups. Participants have to be persuasive, listing the reasons that their opinion is the one that is correct. Part of the process is for each group to be succinct and to influence classmates.

7. After each group has had a chance to present, ask students whether they have been persuaded to change their opinion. If so, they should stand up and move to another group. Follow-up discussion includes what students learned from each other, what they learned about the topic, and what are effective ways to be persuasive.

Sample Applications

Language Arts/Literacy: After reading a novel or short story, discuss *one* of the following:

   o Do you think the plot is realistic?
   o Do you think the author has created characters in the novel who sound real?

o Do you agree with the ending? Is the ending plausible?
o Do you think the novel was true to the period in which it was set?
o Do you think a particular character's actions were ethical?
o Do you think a particular character's actions were a catalyst for change?
o Did you like the book/short story (and why or why not)?

Social Studies

o Immigration
o Child labor laws
o Curfews
o Current events
o Rules

Science

o The teacher asks students to hypothesize what will happen in a science experiment; students can choose from three or four results posed by the teacher or the class, and then form groups based on who supports which hypothesis and why. The students participate in this strategy before the completion of the experiment.
o Eliminating sugar in the school cafeteria

Implementation Considerations

Timing

- Plan for this strategy to take up the whole class period. Depending on the time frame available, the grade and ability level of the students, and the academic content, you might want to introduce the strategy and have small groups prepare their arguments on Day 1, and have the groups present and try to persuade on Day 2.

Design

- You might consider introducing this strategy using content that is easy for the students, so that the first time they use the Barometer they can concentrate on how to be persuasive and support their argument with facts.

Tip

- This strategy is particularly effective for Grades 3 and higher.

How This Strategy Can Support Individuals With Learning Differences

- The Barometer provides a metacognitive structure for students to think through a controversial issue and to use facts to come to a conclusion. Teachers can extend this by asking students to write an opinion paper as a follow up to the lesson.
- The structure of this strategy can appeal to children with attention issues because individual opinions are key, so everyone can choose the group he or she believes in, and there is a natural pacing to this strategy, which

includes listening, considering, changing groups, brainstorming, listening again, and decision making.

- Some children can explain their position better verbally than in writing, and the Barometer affords this opportunity for teachers to assess and monitor thinking skills.

- As needed, the teacher can review rules of a fair debate before the class starts. The Barometer can provide some social skill support for children who need additional structure when discussing their opinions.

- If there are children with auditory processing issues or children who need additional time to participate effectively in a content-intensive discussion, the teacher can work with a small group the day before to do some pre-teaching on the topic of the Barometer. This enables students to bring previously learned information back into short-term memory for purposes of discussion.

Vignette Sample (Sixth-Grade Social Studies)

It is October of an election year, and the students are studying government and the election process. In November, the entire school is planning a mock election in which students can "vote" for their candidate of choice. For this lesson, the teacher decided to use the Barometer strategy. She assessed prior knowledge by asking her students what they knew about the election process in this country. She created a chart on the SMART Board, based on their responses. Then she asked, "How do you feel about the two-party system we have in this country? Do you feel it is the most effective way to elect a president?"

Students started murmuring and whispering to their neighbors, and the teacher knew she had struck a chord with a question that captured their attention as well as their interest. She held up her hand and asked for silence, explaining that they would have lots of time to voice their opinion in a bit. This was the third time the students had used this strategy and they were familiar with the rules, so the teacher just needed to review them briefly. She pointed out the large colorful chart on the wall that indicated which group to join for each opinion (e.g., Group 1 for "strongly agree") and then indicated where in the classroom each group should convene. After giving students a few minutes to decide, she asked them to move to their groups.

There were 25 students in the class. Although the majority went to either "strongly agree" or "tend to agree," there were a number of students in the middle, or neutral, five in "tend to disagree," and three in "strongly disagree." This made it interesting. The desks had been cleared from the center of the room, leaving a big open space. Students were asked to choose their groups, and then each group was shown where to set up their circle of chairs on the continuum. The teacher had planned an imaginary diagonal line from the back left side of the classroom to the front right side of the classroom. She had the "strongly agree" group arrange their chairs in a tight circle at the top of the imaginary line, the back left side. The next group, the "tend to agree" group, arranged their chairs in a tight circle on the line directly below the first group. This continued in sequential order, with the final group, the "strongly disagree" people, at the bottom right of the classroom. This set up, in effect, a barometer: a visual continuum of opinions from left to right diagonally across the classroom.

After everyone was arranged along the barometer, the teacher gave the class 15 minutes to work with their group to make a strong case to support their opinion. Students were reminded to state the opinion of the group and then list the facts that supported their position. The noise level rose as the students discussed the issue with enthusiasm.

After 15 minutes, it was time for each group to state its case. She reminded everyone that the goal was to support opinion with fact and to try to persuade other students to change groups, based on the strength of the argument of another group.

After each group made their case, the students were asked whether anyone would like to switch groups, and three people got up and moved to a different group. The most interesting was the student who went from "tend to disagree" to "strongly agree" because of the strong case that group had made.

A lively discussion ensued about government, the election process, our personal responsibility as citizens, and about the most effective way to support an opinion. The lesson was successful and the teacher planned to use the strategy again.

Related Information and Resources

Barometer—Taking a Stand on Controversial Issues: http://www.facinghistory.org/resources/strategies/barometer-taking-a-stand-cont

STRATEGY 5

Chain Reaction

Explanation

Students stand in a line and the teacher whispers a topic to the first child, beginning a chain reaction. One by one, the children whisper a word or phrase that relates to what they heard from the child before them. This strategy enables students to make connections to different ideas and concepts. It is a variation of the old game "telephone."

Directions

1. Have the whole class stand in a straight line or circle. Give the first person a word or phrase.

2. The first person in line whispers another word or statement that relates to the word or phrase that the teacher whispered.

3. The second person chooses a word or phrase that relates to what he heard and whispers it to the next person in line.

4. The third person chooses a word or phrase that relates to what she heard and passes it to the next person.

5. The last person reveals to the class what was whispered to him or her.

6. Everyone tries to guess what idea started the chain.

7. The first person finally announces to the class the word or phrase that began the chain.

8. Each student in line then reveals aloud the word or phrase he or she contributed, in order as it was passed down the line.

9. Students can then discuss the way the different contributions relate to the big idea.

Sample Applications

Language Arts

- o Upper elementary: a controversial topic such as capital punishment
- o Lower elementary: the name of a character in a story

Social Studies

- o Colonial times
- o A president
- o A geographic region
- o Civil war battles
- o Community workers

Science

- o Global warming
- o Recycling

Implementation Considerations

Grouping

- Keep in mind that you need a sizable number of students in each group so the strategy works effectively. Usually the whole class can participate as one group, but when the class is exceptionally large, you may decide to create two groups. The chain needs to be long enough to have many details and phrases passed and discussed, creating rich review and discussion.
- When two groups are created, it is nice to have children compare responses. This creates another sense of excitement and interest among children while providing more discussion and review of the topic.

Tips

- This strategy differs from the game Telephone in that students deliberately pass different information from one person to another down the chain. In Telephone, participants try to keep the information passed the same from beginning to end.
- You may need to use this strategy a couple of times so that the students understand their role. For a practice round, choose a simple, familiar topic like "food," so they can concentrate on the process and not on the academic content.

How This Strategy Can Support Individuals With Learning Differences

- Teachers can pre-teach information to be shared by reviewing the topic ahead of time with specific children or asking parents to review the topic at home prior to the Chain Reaction game.
- The teacher can reassure students that it is okay to repeat words or share a word or phrase that is off topic during the secret round because students are only guessing connections. This will alleviate anxiety and remind students it is okay to take risks.

- Students can be given the option of just repeating the word they heard if they have trouble coming up with something new.
- Going through the experience twice provides multiple opportunities for children to succeed without anxiety.
- This strategy can provide multiple opportunities for the children with social skill problems to participate effectively in a group activity because the process is repeated and because everyone in the class is encouraged to take risks. No answer is right or wrong.

Vignette Sample (Kindergarten Science)

Mrs. M. taught a unit on the five senses. To see what the children might recall about the five senses, she used the Chain Reaction strategy. She lined up the children at the front of the class. She whispered, "The five senses" to the first student. One by one, the students passed information to one another by whispering. When the final student was whispered to, Mrs. M. asked Sally to tell the class what was just said to her. Sally announced, "Eyes."

Mrs. M. asked the class to guess what the main idea was that started the chain reaction. One guessed things with two; another guessed parts of the body. Finally, she asked Nakita, the first girl in line, to tell the class what main idea started the chain. Nakita exclaimed, "The five senses!" The class chuckled and a couple of students called out, "I knew it!" Then Mrs. M. asked the class to reveal their answers aloud so the class could understand what happened in the chain reaction. These were the responses: The five senses, nose, smell, taste, eyes, eye glasses, see, sound, touch, fingers, hands, fingers, hands, touch. The teacher asked whether all of these answers were connected to the five senses. Gabriella said most of them were but she didn't think eye glasses fit. Another student said fingers didn't fit, but Jason chimed in, announcing, "Fingers are a part of touch."

Then Mrs. M. asked the students to review the five senses again. Students raised their hands and Mrs. M. wrote the answers on the board: touch, taste, smell, hearing, and seeing. Then she asked the students to repeat the chain reaction. The students shared aloud: The five senses, taste, touch, smell, lemons, oranges, seeing, hearing, loud noise, whisper, touching, rough, and smooth.

The class enjoyed sharing their contributions to the five senses in secret and again aloud. The chain reaction supported student participation because everyone had a turn, which created a sense of excitement as children were eager to pass secrets and guess ideas. It also helped Mrs. M. understand who had achieved the objective of demonstrating an understanding of the five senses.

Source: Jacqueline Ahrens, student, Rider University, Lawrenceville, NJ (personal communication).

STRATEGY 6

Classification Capers

Explanation

Students are given objects, pictures, or word cards related to a given topic. They are charged with sorting these objects into groups based on whatever criteria they decide. The emphasis is on how the objects in each assemblage relate to one another.

Materials

- Objects, pictures, and/or word cards related to a given topic (15 to 20 per group)
- One shoebox per group

Advance Preparation

1. Choose a topic for the strategy.

2. For each group of students, assemble 15 to 20 items relating to the topic and place them in a shoebox.

Directions

1. Divide students into groups of three to five.

2. Give each group a shoebox filled with objects, pictures, and/or word cards.

3. Ask the students to decide how to classify the contents of their shoebox. They can use any criteria they choose, so long as they can explain the system they used. They can end up with as many or as few groupings as they feel they need, so long as each object has a place. Give them 10 to 15 minutes to move the objects around and arrange them into meaningful groups. Encourage children to talk to each other throughout the classification process to debate why a particular object belongs in a particular group.

4. When the classification process is complete, ask each group to share their work with the class and explain how the objects in each category are related. The emphasis is on how the objects relate to each other and what they have in common.

5. After all groups have shared, you can use this opportunity to introduce new words or concepts to the class. You can then direct students to look back at their objects and see whether they can reclassify them using the new terms.

6. Alternatively, when all groups have shared their work, you can ask the class to list all the things they know about the topic, based on what they just did. Or, each group can be called on to list three key facts on the board, and the class can then review what is written.

7. Depending on time, grade level, ability level, and content, you could also end this strategy by following both #5 and #6 above as closure.

Sample Applications

Language Arts

- ○ A story or novel
- ○ The use of descriptive language

Social Studies

- ○ The Industrial Revolution
- ○ Community helpers

Science/Health

- o The five senses
- o Nutrition; the food pyramid
- o Rocks

Variation

When the groups share their work with the class, you may ask the other children to guess how each group of objects was categorized and explain their thought process. The children will come to realize that more than one answer works.

How This Strategy Can Support Individuals With Learning Differences

- This strategy supports children with a low experiential base because they are provided with concrete objects to discuss, describe, and categorize. The strategy calls on the children to rely on both previous knowledge and on the information they construct using the materials provided in the shoebox. In this instance, the preference is to use objects, supplemented with pictures as needed. If word cards are used, children must be able to mentally conjure up an image that the word connotes, and some may be unable to do that.
- This strategy provides ample practice using language.
- The intention of this strategy is to help children make connections within the given topic. This helps children to learn, to understand, and to remember the content and makes the content more utilizable.
- Students can categorize the materials in the shoebox in a variety of different ways, so long as they can state their reason. The open-ended nature of this strategy encourages creativity and accommodates both lower and higher level learners.
- The hands-on nature of the strategy motivates and encourages attention to task.

Vignette Sample (First-Grade Science)

Mrs. O. arranged her students into five groups of four. Before she gave out the shoeboxes, she reminded the children of the expectations for this lesson. She told them that they had to give everybody in the group a turn to talk, they had to listen to each child in the group, and they had to treat the objects carefully. She explained that by "carefully" she meant no throwing and no eating what was in the box.

She also took into account who to put into which group. She organized the groups so that each one had at least one or two children who were leaders and liked to take charge. She made sure that her children who were very quiet or hesitant to take risks in class (for whatever reason) were with children who would encourage, rather than discourage, their efforts.

Each group was given a shoebox containing several different items. Some of the objects were repeated for more than one group, but each box was substantially different from any of the others.

The following is a list of items that were in the different boxes:

- *A grape*
- *A watermelon seed*
- *A peach pit*
- *An apple*
- *A red pepper*
- *A green pepper*
- *A packet of salt*
- *A packet of sugar*
- *Two Oreo cookies in cellophane*
- *A picture of an ice-cream cone*
- *A small plastic cow*
- *A small plastic chicken*
- *A plastic wedge of cheese*
- *A color photograph of a birthday cake*
- *A carrot*
- *A spoon*
- *A plastic knife*
- *A napkin*
- *A paper cup*
- *A bottle of water*

The groups had a good time taking out all the objects and discussing them. They considered several different categories as they moved objects from one pile to another, trying to decide where they should stay. They categories that various groups considered included the following:

- *Things that are healthy and things that are not so healthy*
- *Things that are red and orange*
- *Dairy*
- *Fruits*
- *Things that grow in the ground*
- *Where our food comes from*
- *Things that are hard and things that are soft and squishy*

When the teacher gave them the five-minute warning, the groups scrambled to finish. They were eager to share their work and to see what everyone else had done. After all the groups had shared, the teacher realized that her class had learned a lot about food and nutrition.

STRATEGY 7

Classroom Box Bingo

Explanation

Students walk around the classroom with Bingo cards containing questions and ask peers to answer the questions. This game provides an opportunity for students to discuss or review content material or interact in an icebreaking or social experience.

Materials

- Paper
- Computer

Advance Preparation

1. Create a Bingo card with different questions in each box. Usually, the game uses the same Bingo card for all students, but you may choose to create several different cards, if you prefer.

2. Print one card for each student in the class.

Directions

1. Give students a Bingo card and instruct them to walk around the class and ask other students to answer the questions, one question per student.

2. When the student answers the question, he or she initials the square on the Bingo card. Each student can only answer one question for his or her peers.

3. When someone has an answer for all questions in a vertical, horizontal, or diagonal, line, he or she calls "Bingo."

4. The teacher or class peers check the card for accuracy, and the game continues until others have a Bingo line or until a Bingo card is filled.

Sample Applications

Language Arts/Literacy

- o Comprehension questions from a story or novel

Math

- o Reduce 62/8 to its lowest terms.
- o Name 3 prime numbers and 3 composite numbers.
- o Name one even number and one odd number.

Social Studies

- o Who was the first president?
- o What is the capital of France?
- o Name one function of the Executive Branch of government.

Science

- o What is one thing you do in your house to help the environment?

Implementation Considerations

- Students may develop questions with answer keys for boxes as part of an assignment or study skill experience.

- Students from a technology class may also create the cards for classes as an interdisciplinary experience. The class that actually creates the cards wouldn't use them because they know the answers.
- One grade may create questions and cards for another class in the same grade working on the same material.

Variation: Introductions and Ice Breakers (Socialization)

1. Make up or find out information about students and place descriptions in each square of the Bingo card (e.g., a person who has two pets, a person who traveled out of the country in the past year, a person who is a twin). Ensure the students want to share the information before printing it.

2. Ask students to walk around and find a person who matches each description. Some descriptions may describe more than one student; it's only necessary to find one person for each description.

How This Strategy Can Support Individuals With Learning Differences

- This strategy supports students with memory issues because students get to hear and write information. They can use this information in the future. It is a very interactive experience that keeps students' attention at all times.
- It also provides positive opportunities for students to engage in conversation, which supports social skills.
- Finally, this is an auditory learning experience that supports individuals with visual processing needs.

Vignette Sample (Second-Grade Community Building Experience)

At the beginning of the school year, students were asked to complete a personal survey. Biographical questions were asked, such as name, age, siblings, favorite experiences, and food preferences. There was one open-ended question that asked for interesting facts or experiences. Children completed this form at home with parents and returned it to the teacher. The teacher made a Bingo card using the student information. She added a few questions that she thought anyone could answer, such as "Name your favorite food."

The teacher distributed the Bingo cards to the students and asked them to walk around the room and match information in the box with the appropriate peer. Students could not have one person answer more than two questions. Students who responded to the information had to initial the appropriate square on the Bingo card. Some squares could be filled by more than one person (e.g., "Find a person with two pets and name them"). The first person to get all the answers correct in a line yelled "Bingo!" The teacher stopped the class and checked that the answers were correct. She then allowed the class to continue, to complete their entire Bingo cards. When they were done, students were asked to return to their seats. The first row of students who had all the answers completed won. After the teacher announced the winners, all students were asked to share information from their cards.

Many different students had answered the pet questions, favorite subject, and activity questions, but questions like "Who went to Japan to visit their grandparents for the New Year?" had only one response and made the class shriek with excitement. The strategy gave the teacher the opportunity to create a class profile for future reference and provided an interactive opportunity for students to learn about each other and build a sense of community. This underscored both similarities and difference among classmates in a positive light.

The teacher was concerned that mixed reading abilities, especially at the beginning of second grade, might hinder the individual success of the experience, but she was pleased it didn't. Although the teacher said she would help anyone who needed help with reading the questions, students got so excited to respond and participate they ran to one another and read questions aloud in pairs or groups, looking for the right response. Noise was definitely an issue. Student voices got very loud and students began to scream out for responses. "Who broke their arm at the beach?" was yelled across the room. The teacher had to stop in the middle to explain that yelling and pushing through groups were unacceptable. No one needed to be disqualified after two reminders, and all students had a good time. Quieter students had to participate because they needed to complete their Bingo card, and those students also had information to contribute to their classmates. No tangible reward was given to the winners; students just enjoyed the chance to play.

Related Information and Resources

Bingo for Teachers: http://k6educators.about.com/cs/lessonplanslea/a/bingo.htm

---

STRATEGY 8

Exit Cards

Explanation

Exit Cards are used during lesson closure to provide an opportunity to assess student performance. Students are given an index card and are asked to write the response to one to three pertinent questions. They submit the cards to their teacher before leaving the classroom. Exit Cards can assess student understanding of content and identify student needs in the learning process.

Materials

- Index cards

or

- Cardstock cut to size needed

Advance Preparation

1. Determine what concepts you'd like to assess at the end of a lesson.

2. Develop questions related to product, process, content, application, or other lesson objectives. Include questions that ask students to reflect on the learning process and their specific needs as a student, for example,

   o What was the easiest part of today's lesson?
   o What was the most difficult part of today's lesson?

- o What did you learn today?
- o What is one question you have about today's lesson?
- o Explain how you solve for x in an equation.
- o What is one part of today's lesson that you would feel comfortable explaining to someone else?

3. Write the questions on index cards, one card for each student, or provide blank cards to students and ask them to write responses to questions you pose orally or on the board.

Directions

1. Five to ten minutes before the lesson ends, distribute Exit Cards to students.

2. Ask each student to write his or her name and the date on the card and work alone to respond to the questions.

3. Tell students their responses will not be used as a test. This will help identify individual student strengths and needs and reduce any anxiety related to responding to questions honestly.

4. Ask students to submit their cards to you before leaving the classroom or moving on to the next subject.

5. Use the cards to identify student strengths and needs and make future instructional decisions. Exit Cards can be used as a grouping tool for the following day for a continuation lesson on the same topic.

Sample Applications

Language Arts

- o Define a noun and give two examples.
- o Why is it important to know the setting of the story?
- o What can you infer about a character in a story?

Math

- o What is the order of operations?

Science

- o Define orbit and rotation.
- o List two ways you can conserve energy in your house.

Social Studies

- o What are the Articles of Confederation?
- o Why was Rosa Parks important?

Community Building

- o Who should you go to for help in your classroom or school if you have a problem?
- o If you saw someone getting picked on at recess, how could you help?
- o Describe one way that you are a good friend.

Implementation Considerations

- One option is to pre-print cards with a designated space for name and date, to save time.
- Two to three questions are typical, with one or two related to content and one related to preference and opinion about the learning process (e.g., Did you comprehend the reading? Did you like the learning activity?).

How This Strategy Can Support Individuals With Learning Differences

- If students have trouble with writing skills, pre-print questions on cards. Multiple choice questions can also support both recall and critical thinking skills for metacognitive and writing needs. For example,

1. What strategy helped you best learn division today? You may choose more than one.

   a. base ten blocks
   b. arrays
   c. mental math
   d. scrap paper
   e. multiplication chart

2. If you saw someone getting picked on at recess, how could you help?

   a. pretend you don't see
   b. call a teacher or aide
   c. tell the children to stop
   d. ask the child to play with you

3. Draw a picture of a plant that has water and sunlight and a picture of one that does not get water or sunlight.

Vignette Sample (Second-Grade Social Studies)

A second-grade teacher was teaching about Rosa Parks. She read the story about Rosa Parks to the class, and discussion questions included "Why did Rosa Parks sit down at the front of the bus?" "What is segregation?" "Why couldn't Rosa Parks sit anywhere on the bus she wanted?" and "How did the law of segregation change?"

Using the Exit Card assessment strategy, the teacher asked students to respond to the following questions pre-printed on cards:

1. Rosa Parks was an African American who

   a. sat down in the white part of the bus during segregation.
   b. protested against high taxes.
   c. was a teacher for African American children in the south.

2. How did Rosa Parks help change segregation laws?

   a. She went to congress to make a new law.
   b. She made people realize segregation of races was wrong.
   c. She asked Martin Luther King to protest and speak to the president.

3. What do you think about segregation?

> *The next period was lunch. In order for students to get a pass to leave the classroom, they had to complete and hand the teacher an Exit Card.*
>
> *From the Exit Card analysis, the teacher learned all students understood who Rosa Parks was, and they all agreed segregation was wrong. Some students answered the second question incorrectly. Before beginning the next Social Studies topic, the teacher was able to ask peers to share responses and discuss how segregation laws changed. In her own assessment, the teacher individually asked the four students who got this answer wrong to explain their new responses to her. This strategy enabled her to differentiate her instruction and assessment by re-teaching and only assessing the concept specific students did not understand. The Exit Cards worked as a tool to reinforce reflection and assess student learning.*

Related Information and Resources

Exit Cards: http://www.saskschools.ca/curr_content/mathcatch/mainpages/assess_tools/exit_cards1.html

STRATEGY 9

Fishbowl

Explanation

In this strategy, one group of students—the fish—are observed in an activity by the spectators: those students sitting outside the circle looking into the "fishbowl." The group of students who are observing then make comments about the performance of the inner group. Groups can change roles.

Directions

1. Place a group of students (the fish) in the center of the room.

2. Ask these students to perform a role play.

3. Create an outer circle of students (around the fishbowl) who will observe and make recommendations to improve the role-play situation.

4. If time allows, or the teacher desires, the two groups may switch places and roles.

Sample Applications

Language Arts

Inner Circle: Act out responses to the following, based on the story the class just finished reading:

- o How do different characters in the story react to new situations?
- o Create a new ending to the story.

Outer Circle:

- o What would you do the same or differently?
- o How can you improve the outcome of the role play?

Social Studies

Inner Circle: Act out situations from different historical events such as the Great Depression or the Industrial Revolution.

Outer Circle: Comment on the laws that may have helped individuals in the role-play situation.

Science

Inner Circle: Complete the first few steps of a science project.

Outer Circle: Observe and determine the rules for appropriate behavior during a science experiment.

Community Building

Inner Circle: A new student has arrived in your class. She is from another state, and she has very thick glasses and stutters sometimes. How do the four other students at her table react to her?

Outer Circle: Observe the inner circle role play and comment on each student's actions.

- o Do you agree or disagree with what that person says or does?
- o If you disagree, what should the person do differently?

Conflict Resolution

Inner Circle: Five students are at a lunchroom table. One student is being made fun of by two students, and there are two onlookers at the table. What happens?

Outer Circle: Write down your answers to the following questions:

- o Who were the best and worst communicators? Explain.
- o Do you believe the two onlookers responded well?
- o If you had one of the roles, how would you improve the performance?
- o Do you agree or disagree with the outcome of the role play? Explain.

Implementation Considerations

Timing

- Timing is important. Make sure there is time for role-play groups to finish and for the outer circle to comment and take the inner circle role, if desired.

Design

- Ensure that classroom space allows students in the inner circle to be standing or moving during role play, and have enough space for the outer circle to sit.

How This Strategy Can Support Individuals With Learning Differences

- Provide roles that meet the needs of students with different abilities.
- Provide only one or two questions on a sheet of paper to students in the outer circle, to help students with limited ability or focus issues concentrate on one or two concepts for commentary.

- If students have trouble reading their role from an index card or sheet of paper, the teacher can review the role ahead of time with the student and discuss possible choices of action (pre-teaching).
- Providing specific questions on paper for students to respond to helps provide a purpose, a structure, and a focus for the observers. For additional structure, the teacher may choose different graphic organizer formats.

Vignette Sample (Fifth-Grade Social Studies)

While teaching about the Industrial Revolution, Mr. T. decided to use the fishbowl strategy to illustrate the needs of children working in factories. Role play in the inner circle included five students. Three students were given index cards that read, "You are 11 years old and you work 10 hours a day in a cold coal factory. You have to move coal from one place to another, filling sacks for sale and placing coal into the furnaces. One of the three children falls and hurts herself when she tires at the end of the day." Two other students were given cards that read, "You are foremen who watch the child workers and make sure they don't slack off. If they do, the foreman can fire the children." After Mr. T. assigned the inner circle their roles, he asked them to step outside and work on their act.

He then talked to the outer circle, explaining to the remaining students that they would respond to three questions provided on their handouts: (1) Why did children put up with the abuse of the factories? (2) Did the children support one another at the job site? (3) Would you agree with the choices of the children working in the factory, or would you make different choices?

When the role play began, students in the inner circle watched as one girl fell down, tired and sick. The other child workers tried to help her, until the foremen came in and yelled, directing the children back to work. One boy stuck up for his sick sister and was fired. He had to beg for his job back because his family needed the money. He was beaten and returned to work.

Mr. T. asked the inner group to take a seat and listen to the comments of the outer group. When he asked students to respond to Question 1, student responses included, "There were no laws to help them." "Everyone was so poor; they had to work to eat." For Question 2, most students said their peers did try to support one another, especially the girl's brother. One student said if the other child workers really wanted to support her, they would have all walked out on the foremen, throwing coal all around in a riot. Mr. T. asked the students from the inner circle whether they would change their actions based on the feedback. Only the brother said, "Maybe I should have just walked out, taking my sister with me." Although there were no right or wrong answers, the role play provided an opportunity for students to share perspectives and understand history.

For homework, Mr. T. asked the class to use their text to answer the following question: "How were children eventually protected from unfair work practices during the Industrial Revolution?"

Related Information and Resources

Student Fishbowl: http://www.edchange.org/multicultural/activities/fishbowl.html

STRATEGY 10

Four Corners

Explanation

This strategy provides students with an opportunity to move around the classroom as they select responses to content-based questions. Discussion takes place after students select responses, allowing students to respond to recall questions, problem solve, and share perspectives.

Materials

- Paper or cardstock
- Markers
- Masking tape

Advance Preparation

1. Decide what concepts will be taught during a lesson.

2. Create questions with four possible responses. Questions can be open ended (e.g., Do you agree . . .?) or specific recall (e.g., Who was the head of the continental army?).

3. Write the responses on four pieces of paper or cardstock and tape one in each of the four corners of the room.

Directions

1. Have students congregate in the middle of the room. Ask the question and give students time to think about their response.

2. Tell students to move to the corner of the room that contains the answer they have chosen.

3. Ask students in each corner to discuss their reasons for their response and choose a leader to share with the class.

4. After the first corner has shared their response, ask the class whether they have questions or comments.

5. Repeat so that each group has the opportunity to share and to answer class questions.

6. If a corner is empty, ask other groups why they didn't choose that response.

7. When students are finished sharing, ask whether anyone has changed his or her mind based on the information shared. If so, that student should move to the corresponding corner.

8. Continue with new questions, and change corner response cards as needed.

Sample Applications

Language Arts/Literacy

- After reading a story, ask students their opinions about story events and character choices. Corner response cards may read *Yes, No, Maybe,* and *Probably Not.*
- Put up corner response cards labeled with different parts of speech: noun, verb, adjective, adverb. Read different words (e.g., quickly, very, silly, box). Students go to the corner where the word's part of speech is posted.
- Share a conflict in a story and put up four different solutions for children to choose from.

Math

- Put up corner response cards labeled *even quotient with no remainder, even quotient with a remainder, odd quotient with no remainder, odd quotient with remainder.* Give students division problems and tell them to solve the problem and then go to the corner with the correct answer.
- Label corners with colors or letters. Give students different patterns and ask them to go to the corner with the next piece in the pattern.

Social Studies

- Use corners to identify historical figures such as presidents or explorers, the names of laws or events, or the names of countries and other locations. Provide descriptions and clues and have students identify the correct response by walking to the appropriately labeled corner. Ask students to share why they did or did not choose different corners.

Science

- Use corners to classify animals or rocks.
- Use corners to identify the results of a science experiment.

How This Strategy Can Support Individuals With Learning Differences

- You may want to use a PowerPoint or worksheet so students can see as well as hear the questions asked.
- If a child who uses a wheelchair is participating, leave aisles wide enough for the wheelchair to pass through easily, and keep the floor free of clutter.
- Pre-teach or distribute questions ahead of time to those who need extra support.
- This strategy is effective for kinesthetic learners and students with attention issues because it includes controlled movement with a strong focus on class content.

Implementation Considerations

- You may use fewer than four corners, and simply refer to the activity as "corners." For example, you may want your students to identify long and short vowel sounds or composite and prime numbers. In both of these cases, only two corners are utilized.

- If chaos arises during the strategy, restore order by creating teams or pairs of students in the class. Ask the question, have the team or pair discuss the answers and come to an agreement; then, the team leader walks to the corner of the room that reflects the team's choice.
- When you create questions, consider creating one set of responses that will work for several different questions.

Vignette Sample (First-Grade Language Arts)

A first-grade teacher read Duck for President *by Doreen Cronin as the students sat on the carpet at the front of the room. She then asked them to stand and look around the room. She had placed posters in the four corners of the room that read Yes, No, Maybe, and Probably Not.*

She asked the class to listen to her statement and move to the number that matched their opinion best. The first statement was, "I really liked this book." Children quickly moved to "Yes" and "No." The next statement was, "It was a good idea to kick Farmer Brown off the farm." Most of the children went to "Yes" and "No," but three went to "Probably Not." The teacher asked the students in each corner for their opinions. One student in the "Probably Not" corner said, "The duck should have talked to the farmer first because it made more work for the other animals." The teacher asked, "Based on Joseph's response, who might want to change their opinion and move to another corner?" No one moved.

The next statement was, "The duck was a very hard worker." All the children moved to "Yes." The teacher asked, "How do you know he worked so hard?" Students recounted scenes from the book with the duck sitting at his desk tired, with a pen and covered with ink. One boy said, "He worked and had no fun." The next statement was, "The duck was good at running for office but not at working in the office after he won." Student reactions were very mixed. There were students in every corner, and many looked to see where friends were and kept moving. Then, the teacher said, "When I count to three, you must stay in your corner." Students were in each of the four corners. A hearty debate then began about the capabilities of the duck. One girl said, "He was very good at working, so everyone kept voting." Another girl said, "He was no good, and he kept running away."

Finally, the teacher said, "I have one more statement: Once I thought my friend had better things and more fun than me, and then I found out it wasn't true. We were alike." The students were confused and the teacher repeated the statement. Students moved to "Yes" and "No." The teacher asked students to share their experiences. In closure, she said, "Do you think the duck learned something, like you did?" It was Joseph who summed nicely, "He always wanted more, but it wasn't any better. He shouldn't have moved in the first place."

In this activity, the teacher created an opportunity with movement that provided a new way for students to infer, problem solve, and draw conclusions. By choosing a corner, each student had a voice, even if he or she did not take part in the discussion.

Related Information and Resources

Four Corners Teaching Strategy: http://www.ehow.com/way_5809507_four-corners-teaching-strategy.html

┌─ STRATEGY 11 ──────────────────────────────────┐

Howdy Partner!

└───┘

Explanation

In this strategy, students research information about an assigned name or topic. Students then walk around the room to find a partner with the same topic, using descriptors but not the actual word they were assigned.

Materials

- Large index cards

Directions

1. Create a list of names or concepts from a learning topic.

2. Assign the same concept to two students in the class. If the class has an odd number of students, assign three students to one concept.

3. Distribute the name or concept to students in the classroom by handing them a folded piece of paper. Tell the students they must keep their assigned name or word on the paper a secret.

4. Give a large index card to each student, and ask students to research their topic and record the information on the card.

5. When students have finished recording information on their cards, explain they are going to walk around the room and find their partner *without* using their assigned word or name. Students can refer to their index cards, but they cannot share index cards at this time.

6. The students walk around the room greeting one another and asking questions, such as "Were you ever a president of the United States?" If the other student responds "No," they move on. If the other student responds "Yes," the students continue to ask questions until they learn whether they have found their partner who was assigned the same name or concept.

7. When students find their partner, they sit together and share the information on their cards as they wait for the other partners to match.

8. When all partners match, ask each pair to talk about their topic, using the clues from the cards without mentioning the concept or term specifically.

9. Students in the class try to guess the concept or name being described. If they don't guess it after pairs have shared all their information, the partners tell the class who or what it is.

10. Each pair continues until everyone has had a chance to share.

Sample Applications

Language Arts

- o Vocabulary words and definitions
- o Characters and characterization
- o Information for essays

Social Studies

- o Names of historical figures
- o Historical events
- o Current events
- o Geography of a country or region
- o Cultures and religions

Science

- o Names of scientists
- o Types of rocks or land formations
- o Global warming and environmental study topics

Implementation Considerations

- Students may receive their secret name on a folded, stapled paper or in an envelope.
- Consider alternative activities if students have to wait a long time for their classmates to find their partners.
- To help students stay focused on other groups sharing, one group has to say something about another group's topic before they begin their own share.

How This Strategy Can Support Individuals With Learning Differences

- Students can work in pairs.
- Graphic organizers or sentence starters can be substituted for blank index cards.
- More and less complicated topics can be assigned to students, at the appropriate functioning level.

Vignette Sample (Fifth-Grade Social Studies)

Ms. D. tells the class they are going to celebrate Black History Month. To learn more about African Americans in history, students are going to play the Howdy Partner! game. She hands out a large blank index card to each student and tells them to hold onto it. She explains she is going to give each of them a slip of paper with the name of a famous African American on it. Then, she tells the class that when they receive the paper, they are not to share it with anyone; otherwise they will not be able to participate in the activity. She then takes out a bag and pulls out pieces of paper stapled together. The students' names are written on the outside of the papers. Once everyone has received a piece of stapled paper, she asks students to open up their paper and read the name on it without letting anyone else see. She then tells the students they need to find out information about the person they've been assigned and fill the index card with information. She makes this a homework assignment, explaining to children they can use books or the Internet for research. Most important, she tells them, "Don't tell your classmates who you have, or you will not be able to play the game tomorrow."

The next day during SS period, Ms. D. tells the class to take out their index cards of information. Students are directed to walk around the class and give one another clues about their person without telling their name. She called Manny and Coby to the front of the room to set an example. She told Manny to greet Coby with a handshake and a "Howdy partner!" Coby reciprocated with a handshake and a "Howdy partner!" Coby gave the first clue: "My person lived in Alabama." Manny said, "So did mine! My person sat on a bus in the wrong seat!" and Coby replied, "Too bad, you're not my partner," and moved on. Once students grasped the idea of the game, they were asked to take their cards and walk around the room looking for the right partner as they shared descriptors and information. When two partners found each other, they were told to go to the carpet and share all the information from their cards as they waited for the other partners to pair.

When all the students were paired and seated on the carpet, Ms. D. called the pairs up to the front of the carpet one by one. She said, "Howdy partners! Can you tell us information about your person so we can guess who it is?" Partners took turns telling the class about their famous African Americans. The class was able to guess only a few. In the end, the students learned about Booker T. Washington, Harriet Tubman, Eli Whitney, Dred Scott, George Washington Carver, Lewis Latimer, Rosa Parks, Martin Luther King Jr., Maya Angelou, Corinne Brown, Jesse Jackson, Colin Powell, and Barack Obama.

Ms. D. then had partners write paragraphs about their famous African American during Computer class. Each pair had to write at least one paragraph and put a picture on the report. The technology teacher helped students use word processing and pictures from the Internet to complete their assignments. The assignments created a wonderful classroom display for the month.

STRATEGY 12

If I Were . . .

Explanation

One child has to complete a sentence stem based on a given topic, and another student has to make a related comment. This enables students to make relevant connections and practice appropriate conversation skills.

Directions

1. Tell the class what the academic content is for this lesson, and give them a sentence stem based on the topic.

2. "If I were . . . , I would be . . . " is the sentence stem for this strategy. Fill in the first blank for the class, and let each child decide how he or she wants to fill in the second blank.

3. Students sit in a circle. Child 1 completes the sentence stem.

4. Child 2 is the student sitting to the right of Child 1. Child 2 responds, in one sentence, with a fact that relates to what the first child said (e.g., Child 1: "If I were a plant, I would be a cactus." Child 2: "Cactus grows in the desert," or "Cactus grows best in a dry climate," or "Cactus grows pretty flowers").

5. After Child 2 responds, it is her turn to be Child 1 and complete the sentence stem. The child to her right takes on the role of Child 2 and responds

to her sentence. This continues around the circle until everyone has had the chance to be both Child 1 and Child 2.

6. You can use the same sentence stem as the children go around the circle, or you can change the sentence stem partway through.

7. When the class is finished, ask children to review what they have learned. This can take the form of one of the following:

   o a group discussion (possibly incorporating the Whip, another strategy from this chapter),
   o a list the teacher writes on the board with the whole class contributing,
   o student pairs listing what they have learned on poster boards hung around the room,
   o individuals writing and/or drawing a picture in their journals.

Sample Applications

Colors

   o Child 1: "If I were a color, I would be yellow."
   o Child 2: "The sun is yellow."

Nutrition

   o Child 1: "If I were a vitamin or a mineral, I would be calcium."
   o Child 2: "Milk has calcium."

Community Helpers

   o Child 1: "If I were a community helper, I would be a firefighter."
   o Child 2: "A firefighter rides on a fire truck with a loud siren and very long ladders on it."

Language Arts/Literacy

   o "If I were a character in the story, I would be . . . "
   o "If I were a poet, I would be . . . "
   o "If I were a book, I would be . . . "

Social Studies

   o "If I were a country, I would be . . . "
   o "If I were a continent, I would be . . . "
   o "If I were a president, I would be . . . "

Math

   o Child 1: "If I were a number, I would be six."
   o Child 2: "Three plus three is six."

Variations

- Instead of doing this as a whole group activity, students can work in pairs. Each pair decides which child goes first. Child 1 can complete the sentence stem, and Child 2 can respond. Then they switch roles and Child 2 becomes Child 1 and they repeat the process. The teacher can keep the same sentence stem or change it each time the children switch roles.

- Instead of specifying that the response has to be a related fact, explain that Child 2 has to make appropriate conversation, specifically saying something that is positive (nice) and that is related to what the first child said. The focus is on saying something that makes sense and relates to what the first person said, emphasizing both listening and appropriate response. For example, if Child 1 said, "If I were a color, I would be blue," Child 2 could respond, "Blue is a bright color," or "My bedroom is painted blue." He still has the option of giving a fact if he so chooses.

- Assign students to small groups, each sitting in a circle. Child 1 starts and answers the sentence prompt, and Child 2 responds with a relevant fact. The next child in the circle adds another fact. This continues around the circle, with each child adding another fact until all the children have taken a turn. The goal here is for each child to add a fact, so that the group comes up with as many correct facts as they can without repeating one. If a child has difficulty thinking of something, the group can help. This is the mental equivalent of keeping a ball up in the air. When they have gone around the circle once and they are back to the child who started, the group chooses another child to answer the sentence stem and the process repeats.

- Use journal prompts as a closure: "After hearing what everyone said I changed my mind about . . . (e.g., I changed my mind about what my favorite animal is because . . .). "Three things I thought were most interesting are . . . " "What I would like to know more about is . . . "

- For this variation, children are sitting in a circle, and the speaker holds a small plastic ball. Child 1 completes the sentence stem. She looks around the circle, makes eye contact with a child who would like to go next, and throws him or her the ball. Child 2 responds to what Child 1 said, takes her own turn completing a sentence stem, and throws the ball to the person who will respond to what she said.

How This Strategy Can Support Individuals With Learning Differences

- This enables children to practice participating in a conversation with someone else and staying relevant and on topic. Although this is an important social skill for all children (and for some adults as well, but that is another story and we will not go into it here), some children need more support in this area than others do. This strategy provides practice listening and responding using a realistic conversation structure.

- To support children with language issues, or other learning difficulties that might make this strategy challenging, the teacher can choose to do a quick review of prior knowledge to bring it to the forefront of young minds (e.g., The teacher asks the children to compile a list of every animal they have studied, and then she poses the sentence stem, "If I were an animal, I would be . . . ").

- If children have difficulty with listening skills and/or with appropriate conversational skills, the teacher can use a T-chart to address these skills before completing the strategy. (See the Vignette Sample below for details on the T-chart.)

- This strategy helps children to make meaningful connections with newly learned content.

- This strategy provides opportunities for rehearsal as students conjure up facts related to the content.
- This strategy supports community building as it gives children the opportunity to listen to and learn about each other. To build on this, the teacher can include more fun sentence stems, such as "If I were a sport . . . "; "If I were a sports team . . . "; "If I were an ice cream flavor . . . "

Vignette Sample (First-Grade Science)

The first grade had been studying animals for the past two weeks. On Tuesday, Mrs. P. asked her class to bring their chairs into a circle. She placed an easel with a chart on it between her chair and the child sitting next to her, angling it so that all children could see it.

After she introduced the strategy "If I were . . .", she used a T-chart to remind children how we listen to our classmates and respond appropriately to what they say (see example below).

She asked the children what good listening and responding look like, and they looked at her with blank expressions. Sammy replied loudly, "I don't know," and Samantha drew pictures in her notebook and effectively ignored Mrs. P.'s question. To jumpstart their thinking and add some humor to the situation, Mrs. P. pantomimed someone who was obviously not listening. First, she took a seat in one of the children's desks. Then she looked out the window, started humming, and then turned in her seat to talk to the child behind her. The students giggled, and the teacher asked, "Does this look like good listening and responding?" Without hesitation this time, they all shouted, "No!"

"Hmmm" she said. "Well, if that does not look like good listening and responding, what does? How about . . . " and she gave an example. They murmured agreement, and then hands began to rise. The children came up with ideas that filled the chart below.

Next, Mrs. P. asked what good listening and answering sounds like. Again, she acted out the opposite, this time calling out, "I can't wait till the next snow day" in response to the sentence "If I were a color, I would be green." As the class giggled again, she asked "Well, what if I say, I think green is a very ugly color?" More laughter. "Is this a good way to respond to my classmates, do you think?" And again, the class shouted, "No!"

They filled in the next part of the chart, to give examples of what good listening and responding sound like. Their answers are recorded below.

T-CHART

- Topic: How We Listen Well to Our Classmates and Respond Nicely to What They Say
- What it looks like

  - Smiling at the person who is talking
  - Nodding at the person who is talking
  - Looking at the person who is talking
  - Facing in the right direction

- What it sounds like

  - I like dogs too.
  - I did not know that before.
  - Dogs bark.
  - A dog is a mammal.
  - My dog is named Scrappy and he is brown and white.
  - Maybe your dog and my dog can play together.

After the class reviewed the chart they created, Mrs. P. reminded the children to pay attention to how they listen to their peers and respond to what they are saying. Mrs. P. chose Kim to start. Kim said, "If I were an animal, I would be a kangaroo." Katrina, the child to her right, said, "Kangaroos jump high." "Good job," Mrs. P. responded. Then it was Katrina's turn, and she said, "If I were an animal, I would be a lion." Mrs. P. prompted Juan, who was sitting to Katrina's right, and he smiled and said, "Then you would roar all of the time."

They continued around the circle until every child had a turn finishing the sentence stem and responding to a classmate. Two children had difficulty thinking of what to say, and they were told to ask a friend for assistance, which they did happily in both cases. When the class finished, Mrs. P. asked what they learned from the circle. She then praised the class. She told them their work was very good, that not only did they show how much they learned about animals, but they also did a nice job of listening and responding to their classmates.

Related Information and Resources

Correa-Connolly, M. (2004). *99 activities and greetings: Great for morning meeting . . . and other meetings, too!* Turner Falls, MA: Northeast Foundation for Children.

STRATEGY 13

Information Rings

Explanation

Using index cards and key rings, students create their own information rings that provide review and reinforcement of academic content from any discipline, particularly that which has to be learned to automaticity.

Materials

- Index cards
- Hole punch
- Markers

or

- Information printed on paper (and glue)
- Key rings (buy from a dollar store, or send a note home at the beginning of the year and ask parents to send in any extra key rings they may have in the house)

Advance Preparation

1. Identify the learning objectives related to key concepts for the content area, and decide on the information you want students to put on the cards. Students will be putting together their own information key rings.

2. Decide how students will obtain the content for their information cards. The teacher can disseminate the information, or the students can research the necessary information.

Directions

1. Distribute the materials for students to create their information cards. Information may be written or cut and pasted from word processor documents. It is important that the students create the cards themselves.

2. Instruct students to put a term on one side of the card with the corresponding information on the back of the same card (e.g., a vocabulary word goes on the front and the definition of that word goes on the back of the same card).

3. Students punch a hole in one corner of the card and attach the cards to a key ring. Yarn, twist ties, or pipe cleaners may be used as substitutes for key rings.

4. Cards may be laminated for durability and permanent use.

5. Individually, in pairs, or in groups, students can use the cards to study the terms.

Sample Applications

Language Arts/Literacy

- o Vocabulary words from short stories or novels
- o Sight words (e.g., one side of the card can have a picture, a sentence using the word to provide a context clue, or can be left blank)
- o Parts of a story (e.g., the word "setting" on the front and the definition of it on the back)

Math

- o Times tables
- o Addition facts
- o Math terms and symbols (e.g., the sign " = " on the front and the word "equals" on the back)
- o Money (e.g., picture of a penny on the front and "one cent" on the back)

Social Studies

- o Names of famous people on the front and what they are famous for on the back
- o States and their capitals

Science

- o Science vocabulary words
- o Scientists on the front and what they have invented or accomplished on the back

Implementation Considerations

Grouping

- This can be used with individuals or small groups.

Design

- Depending on the content used, you may want to put information on only one side of each card (e.g., spelling words or sight words).

Application

- Information key rings can both enhance and provide a model for effective study skills.
- This is an in-class strategy that can easily be transitioned for use in the home.

How This Strategy Can Support Individuals With Learning Differences

- Teachers can prepare the information for the key rings to meet individual levels and learning needs as each student constructs his or her own key ring. There is no stigma attached because everyone has a key ring and the differentiation (different words or content) is not obvious.
- Many skills need to be learned to automaticity, and information rings provide the opportunity for needed practice and review, which is particularly important for children with learning needs. Repetition helps content move from short-term to long-term memory for efficient retrieval. This supports memory.
- Information rings support students with organizational skill deficits because, once constructed, the key ring is self-contained, with no loose papers to lose or drop.
- The tactile nature of the information ring provides sensory input for children who need it. In this case, laminating the cards is strongly advised.

Vignette Sample (First-Grade Language Arts)

A first-grade teacher made a handout of 10 sight words, each in its own box. Students practiced reading them together as a class. Then, the teacher distributed 10 index cards with holes in them and scissors to each child. Students were asked to cut out sight words and use glue sticks from their tables to paste words on the index cards. When they were done, children went up to the teacher's desk individually to read words with the teacher and fasten a ring onto the cards. While students waited for their turn, the teacher asked them to practice reading cards individually or with a friend. When a student approached the teacher's desk, she would not only read the words but check that the words were cut and pasted properly. She would fix any errors with extra supplies from her desk.

Sight words were added to the cards periodically during the year. Although all students started with the same sight words, some students added different levels of cards throughout the year. The teacher was able to send lists of words home so that parents could make cards and review words with them, too.

The teacher was able to address fine motor and literacy objectives with this activity. The teacher did consider having students write their words on the cards, but in the past, because students had such difficulty writing, it was difficult to read the words on the cards. For example, letters were sometimes jumbled or mixed together. Having students cut out the words eliminated this problem and better met objectives. Different word groups differentiated instruction effectively and invisibly.

STRATEGY 14

Job Wanted Poster

Explanation

Based on everything they know about a particular character in a story, or a historical figure, students construct a job wanted advertisement poster with that person in mind. This strategy emphasizes comprehension in a real world context.

Materials

- Paper (e.g., construction paper, poster board, manila folder, computer paper)
- Fine-tipped markers, crayons, pens
- Whatever else you might want to decorate the poster (stickers, pictures, etc.)

Directions

1. Let each student choose a character based on the short story or unit of study the class is working on. You might want to provide a list from which they can choose.

2. Explain to the class about job wanted ads and what they are used for. Discuss the various places these could be posted, including the Internet.

3. Give students a copy of Worksheet 1: Brainstorming (see sample below). Ask them to fill it out, using resource material if needed. Talk about how you can figure out from reading a story all of the things that a character does well and what his or her strengths may be. Explain that strengths can be tangible, like being good at building things; a language-based skill, like expressing oneself orally or in writing; a personality trait, like a good sense of humor; or even a social skill, like how we treat others.

4. As children complete their worksheets and their lists, walk around the class and check work, giving encouragement and helping children who need a bit of prompting.

5. Encourage students to think outside the box when choosing job possibilities. Looking up possible jobs on the Internet is one way to come up with interesting ideas they might not have thought of.

6. When students have finished the brainstorming worksheet and you have checked their work, let them start creating the poster, using the materials you have assembled. See Worksheet 2: Job Wanted Ad below.

7. When the posters are complete, let children share them with the rest of the class, share in small groups, or simply hang them in the classroom for all to enjoy and read at their leisure.

Sample Applications

Language Arts/Literacy
   o A short story or novel the class has read
   o Biographies

Social Studies
   o Past presidents from time periods the class has studied
   o Martin Luther King, Jr.
   o Betsy Ross

Science
   o Neil Armstrong
   o Louis Pasteur

Implementation Considerations

Grouping

- Though this is set up for children to work individually, you can have them create the posters in pairs or small groups.
- Even when each child is creating his or her own poster, you might want to encourage the class to talk through their work with a partner, helping each other to work through ideas, using a classmate as a sounding board.

Timing

- This can easily cover a minimum of two to three class sessions.

Tips

- Soft music can play in the background while students are working.
- When the posters are completed and hanging around the classroom, the teacher can extend the lesson by asking each student to choose one poster that is not his own and answer a series of generic questions based on that poster.

How This Strategy Can Support Individuals With Learning Differences

- As the class starts working on the brainstorming worksheet, ask each child to come up individually to the chalk board or SMART Board and write down one job that people may hold. Encourage the class to think of something that others may not think of. This list provides a visual reference of suggestions for children who may have difficulty thinking of an appropriate job, and it can be used as a jumping off point. If a child needs help with the thinking process, ask her to consider all the things the character can do, and ask which of the jobs listed on the board may fit with those skills and brainstorm from there.

- You have the option to pair children heterogeneously if writing skills are an issue for some.

- You may wish to provide a sample job wanted poster for your class. In this case, choose a character that is not part of the topic the class will be working on, like Cinderella, a favorite sports hero, a recent Olympian, or someone else who they will enjoy hearing about. Consider adding humor.

- The worksheet and the poster template support children with metacognitive issues as they scaffold the thinking process for this strategy, and the metacognitive skills practice can be applied to future tasks.

- This strategy accommodates both lower and higher level thinking as well as concrete and abstract thought. Children can approach this task at whatever level they are functioning, and they can be as creative as they choose.

- Social skill building can be incorporated into this strategy. When children are listing strengths and things that the character can do, they can be encouraged to list the social skills that the character possesses and what he or she is able to accomplish because of these social skills (e.g., make friends, solve problems peacefully).

- The posters can provide an outlet for success for children who are artistically inclined. Children with learning issues sometimes feel that they lack opportunities for their strengths to shine at school. Strategies that use a variety of strengths, such as this one, address this concern.

Vignette Sample (Brainstorming Worksheet)

For this strategy, we have included a brainstorming worksheet (Worksheet 1: Brainstorming Template) for students to use to get started and a job wanted poster template (Worksheet 2: Job Wanted Ad Template) to use to complete the poster. In lieu of our standard vignette, for this strategy we offer an example of a brainstorming worksheet as a student would have filled it out (see Worksheet 1: Brainstorming Sample).

WORKSHEET 1: BRAINSTORMING (SAMPLE)

(This one is complete with sample answers; the worksheet template follows.)

Name: *4th-grade student studying comparing and contrasting*   **Date** _____

Subject: *Language Arts*

Before you begin work on your poster, fill out this worksheet. This will help you think through the process and come up with ideas to create the job wanted poster for your character.

1. The person I am going to write an ad for is

   The third little pig, the one who built his house out of bricks in The Three Little Pigs.

2. The reason I am interested in him or her is

   Our class read a few different stories of the three little pigs and compared them all. I liked the original story the best. I liked him because he was funny.

3. He or she is famous because

   He was the third little pig and everyone knows the story. I heard it when I was a little kid, even.

4. Here is a list of all the things he or she does well and a list of his or her strengths:

   Smart
   Clever
   Thinks on his feet
   Thinks outside of the box (thinks of things that others might not think of)
   He is cute for a pig
   Gets along well with his brothers
   He does a good job of building houses

5. Based on the list for Question 4, here is a list of jobs he or she would be able to do (and I will think of as many as I can, including jobs that I come up with by thinking outside the box):

   A teacher
   A lawyer
   A diplomat
   He could build buildings
   He could be a business person (businessman, businesswoman, business pig)
   Real estate agent like my mom

6. From my job list in Question 5, the job I choose for my person is

   House builder or construction worker (depending on the sophistication of the child's vocabulary)

That is the job I will write the job wanted poster for.

WORKSHEET 1: BRAINSTORMING (TEMPLATE)

Name _____ **Date** _____

Subject _____

Before you begin work on your poster, fill out this worksheet. This will help you think through the process and come up with ideas to create the job wanted poster for your character.

1. The person I am going to write an ad for is

2. The reason I am interested in him or her is

3. He or she is famous because

4. Here is a list of all the things he or she does well and a list of his or her strengths:

5. Based on the list for Question 4, here is a list of jobs he or she would be able to do (and I will think of as many as I can, including jobs that I come up with by thinking outside the box):

6. From my job list in Question 5, the job I choose for my person is

That is the job I will write the job wanted poster for.

WORKSHEET 2: JOB WANTED AD (TEMPLATE)

Job wanted: _____

My name is _____, and I am looking for a job as a

_____ . I will be great at this job because I am able to

(Write a list of supporting skills and abilities here.)

Please contact me at_____ .

(Decorate the poster however you want.)

STRATEGY 15

Line Up!

Explanation

This strategy is designed to be used with sequential content, particularly facts that students need to know to automaticity. Each student is handed an index card and silently has to line up in the correct order determined by the number or word on the index card.

Materials

- Index cards
- Pens

Advance Preparation

1. Decide on your content.

2. Depending on your content, you will need to write one letter, number, word, or phrase on each index card. For example, if your class is working on the numbers 11 through 20, you will put one number from the sequence on each index card for a total of 10 cards, so that all numbers from 11 through 20 are represented.

3. You will probably want to prepare several index card packets at once, depending on your goal for the lesson. They can be laminated to make them more durable.

Directions

1. Choose the number of students you will need based on the number of cards you have, and give each of those students one card. The rest of the class is the audience for this round.

2. Tell the students that without talking, they need to look at the index cards and put themselves in the correct order. Then say "Line up."

3. When students are standing in order in a straight row, they should hold their index cards facing the class.

4. When the lining up is complete, the other students check for the correct sequencing. If more than one group has arranged themselves in sequence, have everyone stay in order, and check each group in turn.

5. Choose new students to do this again, using the same answer cards or different ones, as needed. At beginning of each round, tell the students to "Line up."

Sample Applications

Language Arts/Literacy

- o Word cards or letter cards that need to be put in alphabetical order
- o Individual words, one per card, including appropriate punctuation cards; students must line up to form the correct sentence

Math

- o Numbers in sequential order
- o Times tables (e.g., each index card has one of the products of the 8-times table)
- o Money: students have to put in order a penny, nickel, dime, quarter, half dollar, and dollar
- o Ordinal numbers: first through tenth

Calendar

- o Days of the week
- o Months of the year

Science

- o Sequence of events in the growing cycle of a vegetable, starting with planting the seed and ending with picking the vegetable

Community Building

- o Ask students to arrange themselves in order according to length of hair, from shortest to longest, without talking.
- o After using the example above, have students talk about how they were able to communicate with their classmates nonverbally.

Implementation Considerations

Grouping

- Alternatively, you can give out more than one set of cards at a time, so that you have two or more groups arranging themselves in order at the same time. If you choose, all groups can have the same numbers or words to work with, in which case they can compare sequences when everyone is arranged in order.

Timing

- The amount of time spent on this strategy can vary depending on the needs of the class and lesson content. It can be incorporated as part of other lessons and used as either a motivator or closure.

How This Strategy Can Support Individuals With Learning Differences

- The movement and fast pace of this strategy serve to keep children on task and interested.

- The ample repetition of facts, combined with auditory, visual, and kinesthetic representation of the content, support memory and make it easier for children to learn facts to automaticity.
- Movement that embodies content facilitates learning. In this case, the sequence of the material is both physical, as students take the correct place in line as dictated by the index card they hold, and visual, as they view the sequence of the content in order.
- This strategy also facilitates community building because students are working in groups, moving around to quickly accomplish a common goal. The nonverbal component puts a different spin on how children work together and teaches them to pay attention to nonverbal communication skills as well.

Vignette Sample (Third-Grade Math)

Mr. Q.'s class was studying the multiplication tables. He asked the class to move the desks to the center of the room and explained that they would take turns lining up around the perimeter of the room to practice their multiplication tables. He explained that different numbers of children would be lining up at a time and that this would vary each time. He assured them that everyone would get more than one turn and that the "audience" was responsible to watch the line-up process to see whether all the numbers were in the correct order.

Mr. Q. told the class they would be starting with the 2-times table, and he heard murmurs of "easy" whispered among the crowd. He chose 10 children to get index cards (each card had one of the following numbers: 2, 4, 6, 8, 10, 12, 14, 16, 18, 20) and said, "Line up." The children were told that without talking, they had to line up in order of the 2-times table. With just a bit of giggling, the group quickly lined up. Mr. Q. asked the other children to look at the order and vote with a thumbs up if it was correct or a thumbs down if a change was needed. The class agreed that the order was correct.

For the next round, Mr. Q. announced it was time for two different groups to go into action at once. He chose 10 children for the 6-times table and asked them to silently line up at the front of the room, while another set of 10 children ordered the 6-times table at the back of the room. He said, "Line up," and the children scrambled into place. When everyone was in place, Mr. Q. told them to look across the room at the other group to see whether they had the same order. Then he asked the first person in each group to shout out the multiplication problem they were representing and the answer, and they both said, "Six times one is six." This continued down the line, with each pair shouting out their problem with the answer, until it was verified that both groups were correct.

For the next round, Mr. Q. choose 10 children to represent the 5-times table at the front of the room, and another 10 children to represent the 8-times table at the back of the room. He gave out the index cards and said, "Line up." When everyone was done, Mr. Q. asked the group at the front of the room to look at the order of the 8-times table group and to give thumbs up if they agreed with the order. Then the group at the back of the room gave a thumbs up for the 5-times table group.

Mr. Q. had a few students who still struggled with their times tables, especially when they had to answer quickly. He made a point to give them their turns for the "easier tables," like two and five. He also made it clear that groups were to work together, even though they were not able to speak. Mr. Q. felt that he had kept the attention of his students and accomplished a lot in a relatively brief period of time.

┌─ **STRATEGY 16** ─────────────────────────────┐

 Listening Teams

└───┘

Explanation

Throughout this book, we have explored interactive strategies designed to engage students in their own learning. We freely acknowledge that different types of lessons lend themselves best to different strategies. Listening Teams (Silberman, 1996) is most effective for those times when the teacher needs to use direct teaching, like a lecture approach, to get a certain body of material across. At the same time, the need for student involvement is still a priority.

For this strategy, each group is given one question or issue to report on when the teacher is finished speaking.

According to Mel Silberman (1996), "Listening teams create small groups responsible for clarifying the class material."

Materials

- Index cards, one per group
- Pens, pencils, markers

Advance Preparation

1. Decide how you will group the students in the class. Each group will focus on a different question or topic.

2. Choose from the following focus questions and write each question on a separate index card, one for each small group:

   o List three facts that you just learned.
   o Write down three questions about what you have just learned.
   o Explain how you would apply the information you just heard, or give examples to show your understanding.
   o List a few things that the teacher covered that your group did not know before this lesson.
   o Take something that the teacher talked about and explain it in a different way.
   o Relate what the teacher talked about to something from a previous lesson on the same topic.
   o Write down something you disagree with and explain why; if there is nothing you disagree with, then explain why not.
   o Is there a theme or message to this lesson?

Directions

1. Assemble students into small groups, and give each group an index card with a focus question on it before you begin the lesson. Explain that this is what they will need to answer after you have finished the lecture.

2. Teach the lesson.

3. Give groups a few minutes to collaborate and write out their answers.

4. Let each group take a turn explaining what they have written, and give the class an opportunity to respond to what each group says. This serves as an in-depth review of the lecture. You can clarify information as needed.

Sample Applications

Language Arts/Literacy

   o Parts of a story (character, plot, setting, etc.)

Social Studies

   o The U.S. Constitution
   o The Declaration of Independence
   o Exploration

Implementation Considerations

- This strategy is designed for Grades 3 and up.

Grouping

- Determine the number of groups needed based on age, ability, and level of content. You may want to use four questions but eight groups, so each question is addressed twice.

Timing

- The timing of the direct instruction portion of the lesson will correspond to the topic at hand as well as the age, attention span, and ability level of the class. For example, for a science lesson, you may want to spend the first 15–20 minutes building the foundation of information through direct instruction, then use this strategy to reinforce the content, and then finish with an experiment that demonstrates the process.

How This Strategy Can Support Individuals With Learning Differences

- Providing a focus for students as they listen to the teacher talking encourages both attention and accountability. It affords another way for students to stay engaged during a lesson.
- Listening Teams supports individuals with auditory processing problems because students hear the concept orally multiple times, first as the teacher is teaching it and then again as groups take turns explaining the answers to each index card. As students share what they have written down, the key concepts are repeated once more, this time in "oral bullet points," reinforcing what they needed to be listening for.

Vignette Sample (Fourth-Grade Science)

Mrs. H. taught a 20-minute, content-intensive lesson on matter. She felt that there was a lot of material that they needed to get through, and she needed to give her class a solid foundation of information on which they could build. Because there was so much content and she wanted to make sure that students listened and retained what they heard, she decided to use Listening Teams. She also used this as a way to keep them focused as she spoke.

Group 1 had to list three things that they learned from the lesson. They wrote down that three properties of matter are texture, color, and size, and everyone agreed. They gave another correct fact, and then for their third one, they said that energy changes the state of matter. The teacher asked the class to think hard about that one and see whether they could remember what was said during the lecture. She gave the groups a minute to confer and to write down the fact again.

A few of the groups indicated that they needed to change the answer. When Group 1 conferred, they realized their mistake and rewrote the facts. When the class got back together, Group 1 raised their hands and said, "We changed the last fact to make it correct. Heat changes matter." Mrs. P. asked for a show of hands for agreement.

Then she asked the class whether they could explain why heat and not energy changes matter. She asked them to come up with an example to explain what that sentence actually means. Group 4 was able to do this. The discussion helped the class to not only remember the correct answer, but to understand what it actually meant.

When the last fact from Group 1 was corrected, all three facts were verified and Mrs. H. went on to Group 2. They had to explain, in their own words, some of the things they learned. First they explained the definition of matter in their own words, and then they talked about some examples of matter found in their own rooms at home. Mrs. P. saw another group write down what Group 2 said.

She made sure to give every group a chance to share, and then she introduced the class to an experiment using food to show how matter can change states. She felt that her lecture and the Listening Teams strategy gave the class a foundation of information to make the subsequent experiment more meaningful.

Related Information and Resources

Silberman, M. (1996). *Active learning: 101 strategies to teach any subject.* Needham Heights, MA: Allyn & Bacon.

STRATEGY 17

Outline Plus

Explanation

This strategy is as simple as it is effective. Teachers create detailed outlines, with blank spaces deliberately included, for students to follow along with while they are watching a content-intensive video or DVD. Like the concept of reading for a purpose, this strategy facilitates watching and listening for a purpose. In this era of technology, when video clips have become a common classroom resource, it is important to provide support to students to help them identify the purpose and meet objectives for critical thinking.

Richard Lavoie (1989), in his video *How Difficult Can This Be? F.A.T. City Workshop,* described two distinct types of tasks. Associative tasks are tasks that we can perform two or more at a time, the equivalent of multitasking. Cognitive tasks, on the other hand, are tasks that we can only perform one at a time. The interesting part of the equation is that this differs from person to person; what is an associative task for me may very well be a cognitive task for you. For many types of learners, watching a video is a cognitive task, and taking notes is also a cognitive task. This explains why taking extensive notes while watching and listening to something is difficult for many learners. Using this strategy closes that gap.

Materials

- Content-intensive video or DVD to show to the class
- Computer for typing and printing the outline

Advance Preparation

1. View the video and decide what you want students to remember.

2. Write a sequential list of the information you want students to focus on while watching.

3. Use your list as the basis for the outline; note in detail information, like definitions, that you want to be sure the students learn. Other sections of the outline can, for example, have a heading with a list of four major points; you can write in two and the students will have to add two more. The information to be filled in by the students should be brief (i.e., answers of no more than a couple of words each).

4. For your final point on the outline, include an open-ended question that each student has to respond to immediately after the video is finished.

Directions

1. Hand out one outline per person and review the outline with the class so students know what they are watching for.

2. Explain that the outline parallels the video, and students can refer to the outline while watching. Explain that certain parts are already filled in, and other sections require the student to fill in the blanks.

3. If you choose, you can stop the video at strategic points so that students can write their notes.

4. When the video is finished, students can refer to their outlines to take part in a whole group discussion about what they learned.

Sample Applications

Science

- o DVD on how a plant grows, recycling, or nutrition

Social Studies

    o DVD on how a bill becomes a law

Implementation Considerations

Timing

- The advance preparation is time intensive for the teacher. It takes a while to complete the outline, often due to the need to keep stopping and starting the video to capture definitions, quotes, and so on. Once it is finished, however, you have it available for subsequent classes with no more effort than printing a computer file.

Design

- The ability of your students will determine the extent to which you include blank spaces on the outline. The final open-ended question should be included for all students.

How This Strategy Can Support Individuals With Learning Differences

- Outline Plus is particularly useful in the inclusive classroom because it addresses the needs of a multitude of learners, especially those for whom taking notes is a cognitive task. At the same time, it provides support for all learners and does not single out any one student.
- This is especially helpful for children who have auditory processing issues and have difficulty getting the information quickly when the only input is auditory. When information is presented in the form of a video or a DVD, it can be difficult to process and remember the key facts.
- The format of the outline is helpful for children with visual processing issues as well, particularly if you take the time to boldface key words and use a font that is easy to read. The structure of an outline is generally reader friendly and easy to access visually.
- This strategy pairs auditory input from the video with the visual input of the outline and the video, which supports a variety of learners.
- The outline helps students to stay focused on what is most important and what they need to pay attention to. Children with a variety of learning disabilities often have difficulty knowing what parts to attend to when a large body of material is presented without any organizational structure.
- Completed outlines make wonderful study guides. This strategy models effective study skill practices for students.

Vignette Sample (Fifth-Grade Social Studies)

As part of their unit on slavery, Mr. Q. showed his fifth-grade class a DVD on the Underground Railroad. Over the weekend, he made an outline for his students so they could follow along in sequential order and know what to focus on while watching. He also wanted to be sure that they understood the purpose of the Underground Railroad and why it got its name. The terms defined included Underground Railroad, abolitionist, conductor, and station master.

On Monday, he gave each student an outline and turned on the DVD. He noticed that students were glancing at the outline as they watched, and during one part, he reminded them that the definitions were already written out for them. He noticed some squirming, but for the most part, the students seemed to be attentive. Not too much was remarkable during this portion of the lesson.

The eye-opening part came during the discussion afterward. Students seemed to have learned a lot from watching the DVD. They answered questions easily and had a lot of good questions of their own. They had taken from the DVD exactly what Mr. Q. had hoped they would. They were able to explain exactly why it was called the Underground Railroad even though there were no tracks or railroad cars.

Mr. Q. thought back to the process of making the outline and the number of times he had to stop and start his machine just to write down a quote or write about the role William Lloyd Garrison played in liberating slaves. Then he thought of the diverse learners in his class and some of the learning issues each one of them presents. How could he expect them to remember all of the key facts from the DVD by watching it once with no additional input?

He silently concluded that his preparation time was worth the effort, as he reminded his students to keep the outlines to study for their test the following week. And he made a note to himself to share the outline with the other fifth-grade teachers, hoping that someone else would make up the outline for the DVD for the following unit.

What Mr. Q. found most interesting was the reaction of his students. He developed the outline because he had a number of diverse learners in his class with issues ranging from auditory processing issues to inattention and inability to focus. He trusted that the outline would be particularly useful for these students. He was unprepared for the positive response from other students as well, who let him know how helpful it was to have a visual to follow along with.

STRATEGY 18

Paper Pass

Explanation

This strategy provides an opportunity to share perspectives and frames of reference. Students write responses to specific queries on a paper and pass their responses to their peers for comment. Students have the opportunity to share, agree, and disagree with one another.

Materials

- Paper with numbered questions (pictures, political cartoons, or other images may be used in lieu of questions)

Directions

1. Ask students to create study questions (or you may develop questions) related to the content area. Choose approximately five different questions or images for students to respond to.

2. Make up multiple question sheets and number the questions. Make up as many as needed so that all students respond to five questions. For example, if there are 25 students in the class, have 5 copies of each of the 5 questions.

3. Distribute one paper with one question on it to each student. Make sure five students in a row have different questions. Then distribute the next five questions to the next group of students.

4. Ask students to read and respond to the question in front of them. They do not need to identify themselves in their responses.

5. Provide sufficient time for students to respond to questions and then signal the passing of papers.

6. Each student passes the paper to the person behind her, and that person is given time to respond to the new question until the transition signal is made.

7. When all students have had the opportunity to respond to all the questions, call time and ask all students with Question 1 in front of them to share the answers to the question. Facilitate a discussion of the responses, asking for more commentary from the entire class. You will facilitate the same sharing experience for each question.

Sample Applications

Language Arts/Literacy

o Persuasive essays/arguments: Students may comment on school rules, lunch, fields, new course designs, and so on. As papers are passed, others may agree, disagree, and debate.

o Plot development: Students are given a sentence or paragraph to start a story. They then make a contribution to the story and pass it on. When the story is passed to the next few students, explain that students must create details such as a conflict and a resolution, or they may build characterization, develop a setting, and so on.

o Drawing conclusions: Students are given the beginning of stories and are asked to contribute to the ending. Students share their stories with the class when complete and hand in the assignment for assessment purposes. An interesting twist here would be to use the same story starter for more than one group, and then compare how differently the stories turn out. Students can discuss what elements were added to each story that created the variation.

o Parts of speech: Students add to groups of adjectives, nouns, pronouns, and so on.

Math

o Problem-solving questions or a long math equation may be solved and checked as students complete parts and check each other's work.

Social Studies

- o Students may write about choices and opinions related to political candidates and positions on war, economics, and so on.

Implementation Considerations

- Paper pass provides an opportunity for students performing at different levels to participate without pressure. Even if a student cannot participate, he or she may read what is on the paper.
- Papers are typically passed from one individual to another, but the instructor may decide to create pairs. It is exciting to see the different responses from different people. This activity can lead to a very lively discussion.

How This Strategy Can Support Individuals With Learning Differences

- This strategy supports students with auditory processing needs because it provides concrete visual information for students to read and respond to.
- It supports students with a low experiential base because it allows students to share experiences and perspectives with each other.
- Students with higher aptitudes may contribute at a greater intellectual level.

Vignette Sample (Third-Grade Social Studies)

In a unit titled Our Community, students identified different types of communities, such as urban, suburban, and rural. Then they shared information about community helpers, resources, and experiences. The following seven questions were placed on different colored paper. Each paper was copied four times. There were a total of 27 children in the class.

- *Describe an urban community.*
- *Describe a suburban community.*
- *Describe a rural community.*
- *Name a resource in your community and how it helps people.*
- *What is your favorite thing about your community?*
- *How can you help your community?*
- *What would you like to change about your community and why?*

The teacher told the students to clear their desks and take out a pencil or pen. She placed the colored papers on the desks with the writing face down. Each paper was numbered on the back also. Students were asked to read their questions silently and write an answer. If they needed help, they were to raise their hands and the teacher would respond individually at their desks. The teacher then told them to turn the paper over and begin. She told them to work for five minutes. After students began writing responses, she waited several minutes and said, "You will need to finish up in one more minute and pass your paper to the person behind you." She waited, flicked the lights, and had the students pass their papers back. She asked students to then respond to the new question on the paper they received. The process continued for about 30 minutes. It seemed that for the first three questions, the students couldn't think of much to add after the second or third student, so the teacher said to share anything related. Some students named cities like Philadelphia to describe urban areas. Others drew pictures such as farms and ears of corn for rural areas. The most common student response was "I can't think of anything. Someone took my answer." The teacher just tried to encourage them to respond by agreeing or disagreeing.

After about 20 minutes of paper passing, the teacher said, "When you get the next paper we will stop this activity. All students with paper one, raise your hand." One student was asked to read out the answers on her paper. The class was asked to agree or disagree. Two other students were asked to share any other responses not mentioned. The rest of the class was asked what they thought about the answers. A small debate ensued when some students identified their hometown as both urban and suburban. The most engaging discussion was about the favorite parts and the things children wanted to change about the community. Some answered, "We need more soccer and baseball fields." Others liked the libraries and parks. Ways to help the community included recycling, going to school, and following the rules on the bus. The teacher was satisfied that students understood the content. They could also relate it to themselves and share different perspectives about their community, making meaningful connections to unit objectives. All students participated. Some were not able to respond to every question that they received, but most students were able to give some response or wrote, "I agree." In those cases, the teacher encouraged them to write "I agree because . . ."

The best part was that each student responded to the questions, when usually only the same five or six would be very vocal in a discussion. As the teacher walked around the classroom, she made sure to identify specific student answers. She then encouraged typically reticent students to share. For example, one quieter student was proud to elaborate when the teacher said, "Helping old people is a great way to help your community. Who wrote that? How might you help old people?" The student beamed and said, "Be nice; don't get mad on line in the supermarket if they are slow."

The next week, the teacher used the paper pass to reinforce parts of speech. Papers with common nouns, proper nouns, verbs, adverbs, and possessive pronouns were passed around. Students had one minute to write as many words on the paper as they could. Then they put their words on the board and decided as a class which responses were correct. The students clearly understood the strategy and were eager to apply it to another concept in another area.

┌ STRATEGY 19

People Movers

Explanation

In this strategy, students move around the room to create visual representations of different lesson concepts. It is a kinesthetic approach that enables students to use one another as part of guided and independent practice.

Directions

1. Decide when student movement can create visual representations of lesson concepts.

2. After lesson concepts are taught (e.g., patterns), ask students to physically create an example (e.g., Ask students to create an AB pattern by moving

their peers into a pattern formation. Students may line up in a boy, girl, boy, girl formation).

3. Ask the rest of the class whether they agree with the visual representation.

4. If students disagree with the student placement, they may move students around and explain why.

Sample Applications

Language Arts/Literacy (lower elementary)

  o Letter recognition: When the teacher calls out a letter, small groups of students lie on the ground and make the letter shape with their bodies.
  o Sound recognition: When the teacher calls out a sound (e.g., she makes the short sound of "th"), students have to create the corresponding letters with their bodies.
  o Spelling: Line up four chairs at the front of the room. Allow students to choose a word from their spelling list on the board without telling anybody which word they've chosen. Students will use configurations cues to represent the word; for example, the first student is standing in front of the chair, the second student is sitting in the chair, the third student is sitting on the floor. After reviewing the spelling list, students identify the spelling word "try."

Math

  o Number recognition: Students create numbers using their bodies.
  o Place value: Students are given cards with numbers on them and move according to the numbers and place value called.

Implementation Considerations

• You may ask students to create specific visual concepts (e.g., call out letters and sounds), or students may be asked to create a visual concept and other students have to identify it.
• You need to determine the amount of space in the classroom necessary for students to move freely and create formations. Consider floor space available when asking students to create letters with their bodies.
• Think about the number of groups. Decide whether groups will respond to each other, or all students will respond to each group at one time.
• It is important to do one or two guided practices with students so that the students understand the directions because even with the best estimation, student movement may require more or less space than anticipated.

How This Strategy Can Support Individuals With Learning Differences

• You can ask students to provide less or more difficult representations based on specific skill levels.

- Students can be paired in mixed or like ability groups to support instruction and achievement.
- This strategy supports students who require movement during instruction and those who have attention issues.

Vignette Sample (Third-Grade Math)

Mrs. S. was teaching a lesson on place value. She created four groups of five students. She handed each student one of the following numbers: 1,2,3,4,5.

She asked the students to create the number 13,542. Students were asked to look at each other's groups one at a time to determine whether the groups had arranged themselves correctly. Once students had determined they were in the correct order, Mrs. S. asked the student in the tens column to take one step forward. Group members helped one another with decision making. Then she asked students with the hundreds place to take two steps back. All groups complied, and each group concurred their peers' response was accurate.

When Mrs. S. asked students to create a number in which the highest digit was tens of thousands, one group created the number 5423. The other groups corrected the group by identifying place values from right to left, "Ones, tens, hundreds, and thousands." The group in question immediately added the last number to the end of the line, creating an accurate response of 54,231. Together the class recited the place value of each number as Mrs. S. pointed to the child in each position, beginning with the ones place. Some teacher directions allowed students to create numbers and others asked students to identify place value. Students had to rely on listening and cognitive skills to complete the tasks successfully.

┌STRATEGY 20
Play Dough Construction

Explanation

The teacher gives the class a verbal prompt, based on academic content. Students build something with play dough that relates to the content. When students are finished, they describe what they made and how it relates to the given topic. Some of the representations students are asked to create lend themselves well to each student sharing, and others are better suited to whole group discussion questions.

Materials

- Enough play dough for each student to have a good sized lump
- Plastic knives for each student (optional)
- Rulers (optional)
- Paper towels

Directions

1. Students clear their desks and put down a paper towel to serve as a placemat.

2. You can begin the lesson with a quick review of the academic content and then provide each student with a lump of play dough.

3. Give the class an academic content prompt and then give them a few minutes to create something with their play dough.

4. For prompts that are more open-ended and reflective (e.g., Make something that represents . . .), each student takes a turn showing the class what she has made and explaining how it connects to the topic.

5. For prompts that have one answer (e.g., Divide the circle into thirds), one student can model the correct answer and others can self-check. Discussion can follow as appropriate.

6. Time, topic, and grade level will dictate whether students create one object or more during the class period.

Sample Applications

Language Arts/Literacy

- o Spelling/phonics: Students use play dough to form the vowel in the word "pat" or make the letters that are silent in the word "night."
- o Novel/short story: Students choose their favorite character in the novel the class just finished. They use the play dough to create a symbol of this character and then explain the connection between the symbol and the character. Alternatively, students can create an object that they associate with the character. Younger students can be asked to make something that the character uses in the story, or could use if it were available.

Social Studies

- o Students make an object that is representative of a particular time period, culture, or country.
- o Students create an object that is representative of a story that is in the news currently.

Math

- o Practice math concepts of even, odd, greater than, and less than (e.g., Make an even number of small balls).
- o Fractions (play dough is compressed into a flat circle and children make fractional parts)
- o Diameter, perimeter, etc.

Community Building

- o Students can use the play dough to create something that symbolizes their personality or their name.

Implementation Considerations

- • Frequently, this strategy is considered primarily for young children. It is equally effective for older elementary school students, particularly when the content is more advanced or the questions posed require higher order thinking.

How This Strategy Can Support Individuals With Learning Differences

- Many specialized reading programs (e.g., Orton-Gillingham) that are designed to teach reading to nonreaders or individuals with reading difficulties incorporate multisensory strategies such as play dough as an integral part of the program. As shown in the examples we have included, this strategy is effective for use in a variety of content areas.
- The multisensory nature of this strategy make it particularly effective for a variety of learners.
- Creating with play dough increases sensory input for children who are hyposensitive to touch. If a child is hypersensitive to touch and is therefore uncomfortable touching the play dough, you can put a small amount of play dough in a plastic bag and seal it so the child is touching the bag, not the actual play dough. Another possibility is to give the child a partner so the child contributes to the ideas but not to the molding of the play dough.
- Play dough construction supports children with attention issues.

Vignette Sample (Kindergarten Literacy)

A teacher distributed a baggie with play dough to each child. In a pre-reading lesson related to letter and sound recognition, the teacher told the students to make the letter A. Then, after checking, she asked the students to make an object that began with the letter A. Most made an apple. Some of the more ambitious children made an alligator or an airplane. She then asked the class to make something that started with the sound "d." Some tried to make a dog and one made a door. When children made errors or couldn't think of something, the teacher asked another student to try and help them. Sometimes it was unclear whether the ideas were the individual's or he or she was just copying a neighbor, but at least the teacher felt the skill was being reinforced even if it wasn't the student's original response.

For a challenge, the teacher also asked students to create things that ended with specific sounds, like "t" and "g." These were considerably harder and students were given permission to work together at the table cooperatively. Overall, it made a dry review fun and interactive.

STRATEGY 21

Puzzle Pieces

Explanation

Pieces of related information are placed on different cards, and the cards are distributed to different students. To solve the puzzle, students walk around and talk to each other until they find matches for their cards. Classmates have the opportunity to agree, disagree, and debate matching puzzle choices.

Materials

- Cardstock or index cards
- Scissors

- Glue
- Envelopes (for cooperative activity groups)

Advance Preparation

1. Identify the learning objectives related to the key concepts of the content area.

2. Decide whether to give students the information on their index cards or ask students to research the information and hand it in to you.

3. Print the information on one side of each card. Information can be printed on cardstock that is then cut into smaller cards or printed on paper and glued to index cards.

4. Shuffle the cards before distribution or place them in envelopes for cooperative groups.

Directions

1. Walk around the room handing a card or cards to random students.

2. Give students directions on how to organize the cards, depending on the lesson objectives. For example, they may need to match terms with definitions, sequence story events, or compile True and False statements.

3. Students either work in groups or work with the entire class.

4. Once students have determined which cards match or belong together, they let the teacher know they are ready for evaluation.

5. You may ask classmates to discuss, debate, and defend card choices, or you may evaluate the card matching choices.

Sample Applications

Language Arts/Literacy
- Vocabulary words and definitions
- Story characters and characteristics or quotes

Math
- Mathematics symbols and their definition for use
- Math equations and their solutions, for example, $(5 + 4) \times 2$ written on one card and 18 on the corresponding card

Geography
- States and their capitals
- Map symbols and their meanings

Social Studies
- Information from timelines
- Causes and effects of wars or other historical events

Science

o Vocabulary and definitions

o Names of planets and descriptions

Study Skills

o Students create questions and answers for test questions and submit them to the teacher, who creates the puzzle cards

Implementation Considerations

Design for Research/Inquiry Assignments

- Students may research new information to share with the class and submit information for cards to the teacher (e.g., students are assigned different branches of government and must write about their functions).
- In inquiry assignments, students design their own research questions related to a topic and submit responses for card matching and sharing.

Mixed Abilities

- Information on cards can be specifically distributed based on student ability, to challenge and support where necessary.
- Cooperative groups can be formed purposefully.

Variation: Cooperative Groups

1. Two or more teams may be given the same set of mixed cards with information.

2. Place cards in envelopes and provide one envelope to each cooperative learning group.

3. Each group has to arrange mixed puzzles pieces in an order that makes sense (e.g., terms and definitions, sequencing).

4. Other students and groups may be called on to examine and compare results with their own. Thus, a dialogue ensues to further the student-centered learning experience.

5. When teams are ready, in a class discussion, students review one another's work, comparing and contrasting matching decisions.

How This Strategy Can Support Individuals With Learning Differences

- Cards provide visual support for students with auditory processing needs and language needs.
- Repetition and discussion supports memory.
- Students with social skill needs are provided a structure and purpose to interact appropriately.

Vignette Sample (Fourth-Grade Social Studies)

Student desks were arranged in five groups. Each group had four or five students in it. The teacher gave out a group of cards in an envelope to each group of students. On individual cards were the names of the three branches of government and the different roles of each. For example, students had to match the Executive Branch card with cards that read "the president," "enforces laws," and "commander-in-chief of the armed forces." The students had not seen this information prior to this activity. They were able to use their text or other classroom resources to complete the assignment. Once the groups were finished, students were asked to rotate to the next table to check the card choices. Students debated a few different choices until all groups had correct responses. In the next activity, the teacher asked each student to write a paragraph about the branches of government using the cards as a reference.

In this situation, the teacher used the puzzle pieces to introduce new information on a topic he typically found dry to teach. The puzzle pieces, along with relevant resources, helped students to construct knowledge. It also created a graphic organizer for a related writing assignment. Allowing the groups to check one another's work created an opportunity for the students to move purposefully within the structure of the lesson, debate their peers, and reinforce new information.

STRATEGY 22

Quick Questions

Explanation

This strategy incorporates elements from the popular games of Scattergories and Jeopardy in a strategy that encourages higher order thinking. In Quick Questions, students are given the answers and they have to come up with the questions. A solid understanding of the topic is necessary.

Materials

Paper
Pencils
An answer card for each student

Advance Preparation

1. Think of five words or phrases that relate to the topic you have chosen.

2. Write all five words or phrases on each card, leaving space for students to write a question next to each answer.

Directions

1. Arrange students in groups of four. Give each member of the group the same answer card and a pencil.

2. When you say "Go," each student works individually to write down a question that would be appropriate and correct for each of the answers on the card. Students have three minutes to complete the task (Adjust time as needed).

3. When time is up, students compare the questions they wrote with their group mates'. For each question that the group agrees is correct, all students who wrote down that question receive one point. For each question that is both correct and unique (meaning no one else in the group has written it down), the student who wrote the question receives two points. Scoring can be tallied up by individual or by group.

4. If all groups have the same words on their cards, the teacher may choose to have the groups compare the questions they have created.

Sample Applications

Language Arts/Literacy
  o Possible answers include noun, verb, alliteration, word that has an "n" in it.

Math
  o Possible answers include one foot, one yard, one cup, one pound.

Social Studies
  o Possible answers include Alaska, Hawaii, Ohio, New York, Washington.

Science
  o Possible answers include eggs, milk, steak, bread.

Implementation Considerations

Grouping

- Students can work in pairs.

Design

- To introduce this strategy, let students work in their groups to complete one card per group. To score, they compare their questions to every other group. Keep number of groups to no more than five.
- The teacher can differentiate this activity with multiple entry points by creating one card for Group 1, a different card for Group 2, and a third card for Group 3. Each card will cover concepts or vocabulary that match the level of that particular group.
- Depending on the grade level and the complexity of the vocabulary words, you can choose to spend a few minutes with the whole class on a review of prior knowledge before you give out the cards. Alternatively, review the concepts ahead of time with a small group of students who might benefit from this approach.

Tip

- Model the strategy before students break into groups. You might want the entire class to fill out one card together to demonstrate how to look at one word and write a corresponding question.

Variation

- This strategy is designed for Grade 3 and higher. Second graders can work in a group with a teacher. Give the group five word cards, and for each they have to generate a list of appropriate questions and dictate the list to the teacher.

How This Strategy Can Support Individuals With Learning Differences

- This strategy can accommodate the child with visual processing issues if you take into account the design of the cards given to each student. The individual words should be large enough to read easily, with a font that is easy to read and stands out from the background, and there should be ample space to write the question.
- This strategy works well for students of varying ability levels, particularly in vocabulary and communication skills. Students can write whatever questions they choose, so long as they can explain how they relate logically to the words they were given. Both simple and more complex questions have equal opportunities to earn points. This allows students to use their creativity and to be as challenged as they choose.
- In addition, this strategy provides ample practice for students who have language and communication issues.

Vignette Sample (Fourth-Grade Health and Nutrition)

The class of 20 students was sitting in five small circles of four students each. For this particular lesson, the teacher allowed students to choose their own groups. She explained to the students that on the index cards they would be getting, there were numbers from one to eight, and next to each number was a word. The word represented the "answer," and it was up to each student to compose a question that fit that answer. For each of the eight "answers," students, on their own, were to write an appropriate question on the index card. She told them they had to write questions that made sense and could be reasonably answered by the word on the index card. She also explained that they would earn bonus points for coming up with questions that no one else had thought of.

It took a while to explain because this was the first time the teacher had used this strategy. She gave an example using the word "winter," and asked children to make up questions that could be answered with the word "winter." Hands raised high in the air as the students suggested, "What is the coldest season of the year?" and "In what season does it snow?" and "During what season does New Year's Day fall?" Once students caught on, they worked to come up with questions that made sense and were original.

Once they were off and running with the concept, the teacher was ready to start the strategy. She gave each student an index card and a pencil, said, "Go," and the children turned over their index cards. She gave them three minutes in which to compose their questions. On each index card was written "an eggplant, a tomato, a bagel, milk," and four more words that related to the chapter on nutrition and health.

The following are the questions that Jimmy wrote for the first four answers:

1. *eggplant—What is a vegetable that is purple and shaped kind of like a long pear?*
2. *tomato—What is a salad ingredient that is used like a vegetable but is really a fruit?*
3. *bagel—What is an example of a carbohydrate that is round?*
4. *milk—What is one source of calcium?*

The teacher called time, and there were a few groans. (Some children pleaded for more time, another just said it was really hard, and a few others agreed that this was really cool.) The teacher explained that it was time to share what they wrote with the members of their group and to compile a score. Jimmy got one point each for numbers 1 and 4 because everyone agreed the questions fit the answers well, but Suzy had the same question for number 1, and everyone in the group had the same question for number 4. Jimmy got two points each for numbers 2 and 3 because the questions were rated as good ones, and no one else had written down those questions. Actually, group members were impressed with his answer to number 2 about the tomato. He got a total of six points for the first four, and then the group went on to score the rest of the index cards. There was laughter and high fives as students compared their questions and debated which ones made sense. The teacher had all members in the group add their scores together, and she kept a list of the total scores for each group. For closure for the lesson, she had each group share one thing they had learned that day.

When the lesson was finished, the teacher felt that the students had a good grasp on the content, and she appreciated that they were able to form questions as she realized that this is a higher level skill. She decided that next time she would use this strategy to develop a geography lesson.

She started to think about the students in her class who were at very different reading levels, from far below fourth-grade level to pretty far above. She decided that she could try the Quick Questions strategy with vocabulary words, but instead of giving every group the same words, each group would get an index card with words at their reading level. All groups would be working on vocabulary, but the actual content would be differentiated according to group level. She left the classroom at the end of the day, her head filled with all the future lessons she wanted to try out with her class.

┌STRATEGY 23

Rainbow Ball

Explanation

The teacher creates a paper ball with a question on each layer. Students take turns tossing, catching, and unwrapping the ball and answering the questions.

Materials

- Several sheets of paper of different colors, 10 to 12 per ball (computer paper works well; construction paper does not)

- Pen or fine-tipped marker
- Tape (optional, to keep the ball together)

Advance Preparation

1. Determine the content to be addressed.

2. For each ball, think of 10 to 12 questions, and write one question in the middle of each sheet of paper (or, to support lower level readers, use pictures instead of words).

3. Take the first piece of paper and crumple it into a tight ball.

4. Put the second piece of paper around the tight ball, and crumple that as tightly as you can.

5. Continue with the remaining sheets, taking one at a time and crunching it tightly around the ball you are creating until you have a round mass of paper. The key is to crush each piece around the one before as tightly as you can. The different colors add interest and can be used as a tool for differentiation of instruction (see below).

6. If this will be used for a large group, or if you want to cover more content, create additional balls with new questions. (Ten to 12 sheets per ball is maximum.)

Directions

1. Have the students sit in a circle. Alternatively, they can stay at their desks.

2. Tell students the lesson content so they know the kind of questions to expect.

3. Throw the ball to one student, who peels off the first layer of the ball, reads the question on the sheet, and states the answer out loud.

4. That student throws the ball to someone else, and the process (throw, peel, answer, throw) is repeated until there is no ball left.

5. Student performance (What content did they know? What was difficult?) can influence future lesson planning.

Sample Applications

Math
  o Math facts

Language Arts
  o Define vocabulary words and/or use them in a sentence (see variation below).
  o Spelling words: First child catches the ball, reads the word from the first piece of paper, and throws the ball to another student; that student has to spell the word and then read off the next one for someone else to spell.

Literature

o Questions about a particular story can run the gamut from rote to higher order thinking

Science

o Define science vocabulary words

Implementation Considerations

Grouping

- To use this with a large group, have two or more balls prepared with different questions on each one so that you have enough questions for all students. Alternatively, you can have students work in pairs to answer questions.
- Smaller student groups also work. In this case, you can assemble the number of balls that you need so you have one per group, and use the same questions for each ball. You can then move from group to group.

Timing

- Encouraging students to answer quickly and then throw the ball to the next person keeps the momentum going. Alternatively, for more open-ended questions, you can allow for discussion after each answer (e.g., Did anyone else see this from a different point of view?)

Variations

- Write one vocabulary word on each sheet. The first child catches the ball, peels off the first sheet, reads the word and defines it, and then throws the ball to a classmate who has to use that word in a sentence; this allows two student ball tosses for each sheet of paper and still keeps the momentum going.
- This strategy can be easily differentiated for higher aptitude and lower aptitude learners together in the same group. We suggested, above, that the ball be made up of several different colors of paper to add visual interest. This is also the key to differentiation. Questions can be color coded (e.g., blue sheets = higher level questions; red = medium; yellow = the easier ones).

  o To further simplify, all of the darker colors can be harder questions; all of the lighter colors can be easier questions (simpler for the teacher to remember at a glance and harder for the students to figure out the code).
  o To facilitate this system of differentiation, the teacher has to be a member of the group; the ball is thrown back to the teacher each time, and she chooses (apparently randomly) the next person to throw it to.
  o Alternatively, after every couple of throws, when one child catches the ball, tell the child not to keep it but to pass it two children to the left and back again four children to the right (said quickly and with humor, this enables the teacher to control who gets which color without making it obvious).
  o The key is to do this switching around with humor and randomly, in terms of both when it happens and which student is called on to pass the ball around without reading the question.

How This Strategy Can Support Individuals With Learning Differences

- This strategy is fast paced, and the concept of throwing around a diminishing paper ball is certainly a novel one. The pacing and the novelty create interest and increase student attention to task. The physical nature of the strategy is useful for kinesthetic learners and helps to maintain focus.
- Students of different ability levels can be included in the same group by differentiating the ball itself (see the second variation, above).

Vignette Sample (First-Grade Science)

Mr. P.'s first-grade class is studying animals. He created two different balls to use with his class. Each ball was made up of 10 sheets of paper, with a picture of an animal in the middle of each paper. (Google Images saved the day!) His students were seated in pairs so that they could work together. Mr. P. started off by giving the ball to Samantha and asking her to throw it back to him. He caught the ball and dramatically unwrapped the first sheet. The students were looking at him quizzically to see what was going to happen next. He looked at the paper and exclaimed, "I think it is a zebra" as he showed the page to the class.

Mr. P. then listed two things he knows about zebras and asked the class to put their thumbs up if they agreed the facts were correct, which they did. Then he explained that he would throw the ball to the next pair, who would peel off the top layer of the ball, name the animal, and tell the class a few facts they know about the animal. Students were asked to share between one and three facts. Using both balls, there were 20 pages and 10 pairs in the class, so everyone had two turns.

Students took turns and uncovered a polar bear, a giraffe, a kangaroo, and then a dog. The fifth picture turned out to be a kangaroo again, prompting the children to giggle. Mr. P. remarked, "Hmmm, I think we have seen that kangaroo before. Is there anything else we know about the kangaroo?" He asked this question some of the time when the animal was a repeat, depending in part on which pair was answering the question.

The lesson proceeded quickly, with a lot of giggling and correct answers. As they walked back to their seats, the children asked when they could do this again. Mr. P. is thinking that for homework he can ask the children to cut out a few pictures of different foods, or maybe just fruits and vegetables, and bring them into class, so he will have a head start for the next rainbow ball lesson. (And thinking ahead, he is prepared to have extra magazines in the class for children who might need them.)

┌─ STRATEGY 24 ─────────────────────────────────

Round Robin

───┘

Explanation

In this strategy, students brainstorm and share information about a topic. They rotate through stations, responding to a question and commenting on and adding to the contributions of others. At the end of the activity, students share information from the stations, and the teacher facilitates a strong student-centered discussion related to student responses.

Materials

- Large poster paper for the wall
- Tape
- Colored markers or pens

Advance Preparation

1. Create four or five stations around the classroom by taping large poster paper to the wall or floor.

2. Choose a different topic for each station, and develop material (questions, pictures, headlines, letters, etc.) for the students to respond to at each station.

Directions

1. Divide the class into the same number of groups as there are stations. Ask each group to stand at a station, and give them different colored markers, so that each group's contributions can be easily identified. This encourages accountability.

2. Groups work together to respond to the question at their station, and after a few minutes, students move to the next station.

3. At the next station, students add to the responses or make comments about the previous group's contributions.

4. At the end of the Round Robin activity, a student from each group shares the information from their last station.

5. You can then lead a discussion related to the station responses.

Sample Applications

Language Arts/Literacy

- o Letters or sounds: Write a letter on the poster and ask children to draw a picture or write a word that begins with the same sound the letter makes. When students rotate to the next station, they cannot use the same pictures or words chosen by other class groups. If they agree with the other groups' responses, they can draw a circle around the words and pictures. If they think another group has an incorrect response, they can put a question mark next to it or draw a box around the word.
- o Characters and storylines: Students share and develop descriptions or comparisons of characters and events in stories or novels. They may make text-to-text or text-to-self connections.
- o Tape a picture of a different object on each poster. Each group has to decide on a novel use for this object and describe it in writing on the poster. This facilitates both writing and higher order thinking skills.
- o Word families: Each station has a word family on the poster (e.g., ate). Students are asked to create three words in the word family. Students are not allowed to repeat responses already written.

Math

- ○ Create factors of numbers.
- ○ Respond to word problems.

Social Studies

- ○ Write facts about an event or topic (e.g., Write about the pros and cons of the Industrial Revolution).
- ○ A picture or headline from current events is attached to the paper at each station and students are asked to provide as much information as they can, including personal opinion, about the picture or heading.

Science

- ○ Explain causes of global warming.
- ○ Describe different ways to protect the environment.

Implementation Considerations

- • When designing your lesson, think about your station choices. Posters with colored markers are effective because it is easy to identify group responses and poster paper acts as a visual focus for group discussion.
- • When it is time for groups to move to the next station, transition signals such as lights or bells are helpful.
- • Be sure to walk around and encourage all group members to participate.
- • If you have five people in a group and five stations, you may ask students to rotate leaders within their groups as they move forward to a new station.
- • Cooperative learning discussion takes place within and after station work.

How This Strategy Can Support Individuals With Learning Differences

- • Written responses support students with auditory processing concerns.
- • Students with higher aptitudes may respond more deeply or broadly to a subject.
- • Group dynamic work and movement keeps student attention on task.

Vignette Sample (Third-Grade Science)

A third-grade class was learning about the environment and related issues. The teacher created five stations and created five student groups. Four groups had five students and one group had four students. Each group was given a bag with a colored marker and a sheet of directions. Each sheet had a different number on it, but the directions were the same:

1. *You are Group 2.*

2. *You will begin at Station 2.*

3. *You will respond to the question at your station by reading it, discussing it, and writing an answer. If another group has already responded, you may agree or disagree with the response, but you must give an explanation. You may also add something like a picture, diagram, or comment to support a response.*

4. *Each group member will take a turn as the recorder as you move through the stations.*

5. *One sound of a bell will mean you have 60 seconds to wrap up. Two sounds of the bell means you need to stop and move ahead to the next station. Always move to the next higher number. If you are done early, try to add more information as you wait for the bell.*

The teacher gave the groups a few minutes to read the contents of the bag and asked whether there were questions. Then he asked each group to go to their stations and begin. Stations had questions written on large poster board. The questions were open ended:

1. *What is global warming and how does it affect us?*
2. *How can we help prevent global warming?*
3. *How can we create a healthy environment at home and at school?*
4. *What does it mean to "Go Green"?*
5. *How can pollution harm people, plants, and animals?*

Students wrote responses and drew pictures (e.g., recycling bins, water, hairspray, garbage in water). When they were done, the teacher asked the group at Station 1 to hold up their poster and read it. Students did not get bored during the sharing process because even if it wasn't their turn, their responses were read and they were asked to comment on them. It was easy to identify group input with different colored pens. It was fun to listen to students expand on interesting responses, like a picture of a fish coughing. The artist explained that when we pollute our water, we pollute our fish. They die and we have less fish in the ocean and less food to eat. We can also eat bad food that will make us sick. This strategy was organized well and supported learning objectives well.

Related Information And Resources

Carousel Brainstorm: http://www.readingquest.org/strat/carousel.html

┌─ **STRATEGY 25** ─────────────────────────────

Sentence Starter Poster Session

Explanation

This small group strategy uses sentence starters to guide students to create posters that summarize the key points of a given topic. Each group processes out, explaining their creation to the class as a whole. The completed posters are displayed in the classroom as a visual reinforcer of the lesson.

Materials

- 3" × 5" index cards, preferably lined
- Fine-tipped markers
- Enough poster board for one per group
- Tape or glue

Advance Preparation

1. To make sentence starters, decide on the content of the lesson and whether each group will have the same topic or a variation on the theme (e.g., Will each group report on a different story, or will the whole class read the same story?). Decide whether you need to make up different sentence starters for each group.

2. For each group, write one to three sentence starters for each participant, depending on grade level and complexity of content. Write each sentence starter on a separate index card.

3. An example of a sentence starter is "The setting of the story is . . . " or "The setting of the story was an important part of the plot because . . . " (See below for more examples.)

Directions

1. Divide students into small groups. Depending on the level of the content and the abilities of the class, the groups can be either mixed ability or similar ability.

2. Give each group a topic and a poster board. Instruct them to write the name of their topic in the middle of the poster board. As an option, they can include a picture as well.

3. Give the groups reading material (e.g., each reading group reads a different short story). After reading the story and having a small group discussion, give each participant an index card with a sentence starter on it.

4. Students must complete their sentence starters by writing the rest of the sentence on the index card. The group discusses the answers, and then they tape their index cards to the poster board. Alternatively, they can paste sentence starters on the poster board and write the answer underneath them, directly on the poster board. Students can include further decoration or illustrations if they choose.

5. Each group, in turn, explains the content of their poster to the class.

Sample Applications

Language Arts/Literacy

The center of the poster has the word *NOUN* written in a bright color in capital letters. Students are given the following sentence starters:

- The definition of a noun is . . .
- Two nouns that we use in the winter are . . .
- Two nouns that I can find in my kitchen are . . .
- Two nouns that are found in the zoo are . . .
- Two proper nouns are . . .
- Two nouns that I have heard about but have never seen are . . .

Vocabulary

Each group is given three or four of the vocabulary words for the week. It is fine for some groups to have duplicate words. You can also consider including some review vocabulary words from previous weeks or readings. Vocabulary in science or social studies material works well here. Sentence starters to use for vocabulary include the following:

- o The word _____ rhymes with _____ .
- o The definition of_____ is _____ .
- o I would use it in a sentence about . . .
- o When I think of this word, the first thing that comes to my mind is . . .
- o I can use this word to describe . . .
- o If my friend did not understand what this word meant, the way I would explain it is . . .

Reading

After the group reads a short story or a novel, the name of the story goes in the center of the poster. Sample sentence starters:

- o What surprised me most about the story was . . .
- o I do (or don't) identify with the main character because . . .
- o The point in the story when everything changed was . . .
- o The setting of the story was . . .
- o I think the message of the story was . . .
- o What I learned from reading the story was . . .
- o This story reminded me of . . .

Social Studies

The class studies a specific time period in history. Each group is given the name of a different historical figure from that time period. Possible sentence starters:

- o Christopher Columbus thought he landed in _____ but he really_____ .
- o Vasco da Gama is most famous for . . .
- o John Cabot founded _____ located_____ .

Implementation Considerations

Timing

- This strategy can last from one to two class periods, depending on the grade level and the complexity of the material. The small group work can cover the first class session, and the whole group discussion can take place in the second session.

Design

- The teacher can make up a question sheet that students have to fill out as each group presents. The sheet can have a few short questions designed to help students know what they should be listening for.

How This Strategy Can Support Individuals With Learning Differences

- Sentence starters can be color coded by difficulty or complexity.
- The number of sentence starters per child can be varied according to the grade level, ability level, or complexity of the sentence starters and of the subject matter.
- Sentence starters support metacognition.

Vignette Sample (Third-Grade Science)

A third-grade class was studying the clouds. Additional materials needed for this particular lesson included the science text, printed handouts about clouds, and access to the Internet and a printer for research. This class was given the website www.weatherwizkids.com and told to click on "clouds" for additional research.

The teacher started the lesson by reading the book Cloudy With a Chance of Meatballs, and after a short discussion, she divided the class into five groups. One group was given the topic of clouds (in general), and each of the other groups was given the name of a specific cloud (one cloud per group). The groups started by writing the name of their cloud (or the topic "cloud" for the first group) in the center of their poster board. Under the board, the group was asked to put a picture. They were given the option of drawing a picture or downloading one from the Internet and pasting it on.

Then the groups were given sentence starter cards, one for each child in the group. For this class, the teacher walked around and passed out the sentence starter cards while the children were working on their pictures, so that she was able to choose who got which sentence starter. The children were not aware that her choice of who answered what was very deliberate.

The groups were instructed to refer to their science text and the website provided, discuss as a group, and then individually answer their sentence prompts. After the sentence prompts were completed, the children took turns taping them on to the poster board.

Groups stayed on target, in part because of the way the strategy was structured. Each member of the group participated and had a chance to be heard, both in the small group and when presenting to the larger group. When the posters were complete, each group explained their poster, elaborating as necessary on what was written.

The teacher was impressed with the posters. They were colorful and eye catching as well as a useful resource for information on clouds. When the students went to lunch, the teacher hung the posters on the bulletin board, planning to have the students use the display as a resource during the weather lesson the following day.

For the group that was focusing on clouds in general, the sentence starters were the following:

- *The definition of a cloud is . . .*
- *Clouds are formed by . . .*
- *When I go outside and I see clouds in the sky, it makes me think that . . .*
- *When I go outside and there are no clouds in the sky, it makes me think that . . .*
- *Clouds move because . . .*

The following sentence starters were given to the groups that had a specific cloud to focus on:

- *Our cloud looks like . . .*
- *Our cloud reminds me of . . .*

- *If I had to describe the shape and size of this cloud using only words, I would say that . . .*
- *Our cloud was formed . . .*
- *One of the things that is distinctive about this cloud is . . .*
- *The cloud that is most similar to ours is . . . because . . .*
- *The cloud that is most different from ours is . . . because . . .*

STRATEGY 26

Snowball Fight

Explanation

Students write questions related to a topic on pieces of paper and then crumple their papers into a ball. They throw the papers around the room, taking and answering each other's questions by random selection. This is an interactive and kinesthetic alternative to discussion and review.

Materials

- Paper
- Pens

Directions

1. Ask students to create a question about a topic of study.

2. Have students write the questions on a new sheet of paper, then crumple the paper in a ball.

3. When you call "Snowball fight!" students throw the balls around the room.

4. When the balls land, students pick up one snowball each.

5. Each student takes a snowball to his or her desk, opens it and writes down the answer to the question.

6. Students then crumple the paper up again and throw it around the room when you call "Snowball fight!"

7. Again the students pick up one random snowball.

8. At their desks, each student opens the snowball and reads the question and answer. They write whether they agree or disagree with the previous student's response and why.

9. At this time, a discussion ensues. Ask students to volunteer to share questions and answers from the snowball they have on their desk. The student sharing can agree or disagree with his peers' responses on the paper. Other classmates are given an opportunity to share and critique peer responses. Students who have the same questions on their snowball papers will be able to compare and contrast answers.

10. The snowball fight may end here or continue with another question and answer round. You may use as many subsequent question and answer rounds as desired.

Sample Applications

Language Arts

   o Questions about story elements: characters, setting, problem, events, and theme

Math

   o Solving word problems or equations
   o Asking students to identify geometric shapes and draw samples

Social Studies

   o Comprehension questions related to any topic
   o Community workers
   o Map skills
   o Historical or current events

Science

   o Matter and mass
   o Translucent and transparent
   o Questions about scientists

Implementation Considerations

- If students finish early when creating questions, ask them to write more than one question. If they again finish early, ask them to write an interesting fact or draw a picture.
- Think about transition cues, as the class can become quite excited and chaotic during the snowball fight. Make sure the class is calm and all "snowballs" have fallen before asking students to retrieve them.
- Sometimes one question-answer period may suffice as a strategy in a lesson. If you are just doing review for a test or end of unit, you may use the entire period for snowball questions.

How This Strategy Can Support Individuals With Learning Differences

- This supports students with special needs because it enables students to participate yet remain anonymous while responding to questions.
- Students may use classroom resources such as texts and computers to develop questions and answers.
- If a student doesn't know an answer, it is acceptable to write "I don't know" without being embarrassed.
- Students may work cooperatively in pairs to develop and respond to questions, to support one another and share perspectives.
- This strategy supports students who need movement during instruction. The strength of Snowball Fight is that it incorporates purposeful movement.

Vignette Sample (Fourth-Grade Math)

After the students studied geometry in their Math class, Mrs. R. asked them to take out a new sheet of paper and write down questions related to polygons. They were allowed to use their text or workbook to create questions. Before she began to explain the strategy, she discussed management rules with the class: She told them that after they throw a ball, they have to wait quietly before they move. When Mrs. R. signaled them by clapping her hands twice, students could pick up one ball only and bring it back to their desk. She then told the students they could crumple their papers into a ball and prepare for a snowball fight. She told the students that when she called "snowball fight" they could throw their "snowballs" anywhere around the room.

On the count of three, she yelled "Snowball fight!" She calmed down the excited crowd and asked everyone to find a snowball and respond to the question without the use of any resources. She then instructed the students to throw the balls again and pick one up randomly and respond to the previous student's answer. In discussion, students shared questions such as "Which polygon has eight sides?" Everyone agreed it was an octagon. Two students had to draw a quadrilateral, and they shared their drawings with the class. The fun part was when most students were stumped by the question "What do you call a polygon with 12 sides?" Both students who were asked to respond to the question on paper did not know the answer. When Mrs. R. posed the question to the entire class, one response was "decagon" and one was "dodegon." Mrs. R. asked the students to go to their classroom resources and find the answer. The children read from the text the definition of dodegon and decagon, determining dodegon was the right answer.

Mrs. R. then asked the students to write questions about lines and line segments. By asking students to write topical questions from the unit, Mrs. R. ensured all topics she wanted to review were covered. Finally, she asked the students to write a question about angles, a topic not yet taught. The students had never covered this topic. They explored and read about it for the first time, creating some understanding and knowledge base before the topic was formally introduced during instruction.

Related Information and Resources

Karten, T. J. (2005). *Inclusion strategies that work! Research-based methods for the classroom.* Thousand Oaks, CA: Corwin.

STRATEGY 27

The Spider Web

Explanation

The Spider Web is an interactive activity that has a variety of uses. Students stand in a circle and toss a ball of yarn from student to student, creating a spider web of colorful yarn. As each student catches the ball of yarn, she has to respond to the question that the teacher has posed.

Materials

- A large ball of yarn
- A pair of scissors

Directions

1. Decide on the content area and develop an open-ended question to ask the students.

2. Ask students to stand in a circle. Hold the ball of yarn in one hand and the loose end of the yarn in the other hand.

3. Pose the question to the students, look around to see who indicates readiness to answer, and then throw the ball of yarn to that person while holding on to the loose end tightly. Holding on to the tail end of the yarn is key here.

4. The child who catches the yarn has to answer the question and throw the ball to a student across from him or her, while holding on to the tail end of the yarn. The second child responds to the same question and then throws the ball of yarn, and so on until everyone has had a turn.

5. As the ball of yarn is thrown from one student to the next, a spider web is created and each student is holding a piece of it. At the same time as the web is being created, information is being shared about the topic or content area.

Sample Applications

Language Arts/Literacy

- o For comprehension skills after reading a short story or a novel: What did you find most interesting about . . .? or What character did you most identify with and why?
- o Name one verb (or a noun or adjective).
- o What is the best library book you have read and why?

Math

- o For younger grades: What is something you did at home this week that you and your family used math for?
- o Name an odd number.

Science

- o For a unit on the environment: How does what we just learned relate to your everyday life, or how might you use it in the future?
- o Name an animal and its habitat.
- o What is your favorite healthy food (and what food group does it fall under)?
- o After completing a unit on safety, ask students to share something they do to practice safety.

Social Studies

- o Tell us one thing that you have learned from this unit that you did not know before.
- o Tell one fact about the Civil War.
- o Teacher says the name of a state, and the student who catches the yarn first identifies the capital of that state; then that student names a state and throws the yarn, and the next student who catches the ball of yarn tells the capital of that state.

Community Building

- o As a getting-to-know-you activity in the first few weeks of school, students can name their favorite animal, ice cream flavor, movie, TV show, or the most interesting place they have gone on vacation.
- o After the web is complete, ask two students to drop their strings and describe what happened and why (the web sags because everyone was not holding up their end; this graphically illustrates that every member of the class is important and everyone has to work together). Discuss.
- o Ask everyone to take two steps in and have students explain what happens and why; have everyone take a few steps back, and ask students to describe what happens when every member of the class holds up his or her end of the web. (This is a very graphic representation of the importance of every single class member, and it leads to a worthwhile and spirited discussion.)
- o Name one thing you have done recently to be a good friend to someone.

Implementation Considerations

Grouping

- This is most effective as a whole group strategy with the teacher as facilitator.

Timing

- The objective of the strategy dictates the amount of time needed. The Spider Web can be used fairly quickly at the end of the lesson as a review, or it can be used as a review at the end of a longer unit or as a substantial piece of the lesson itself, depending on both the content and the question posed.
- Using the Spider Web with a more in-depth question or sentence stem and pairing it with asking students to write about it in their journals as a follow up should easily take the whole class period.

Application

- The Spider Web can serve as an informal assessment to determine whether the class is ready to go on to the next topic or level of instruction or whether additional review is needed.

Variation: Collage

As an extension, after the Spider Web, students can use their piece of yarn as part of a collage to represent something they have learned about the topic. Let students write a title at the top of their collage.

How This Strategy Can Support Individuals With Learning Differences

- The Spider Web can support children with attention issues because it allows students to stand, to stretch, and "wiggle" as needed while still listening to classmates, and the growing Spider Web in the center provides a visual focus— something interesting to watch.

- The novelty of this strategy appeals to children with attention issues as well.
- For this strategy, the teacher may need to set up a few basic rules ahead of time to ensure safety and appropriate behavior, depending on the needs of the class. Two rules that are effective here: (1) If room permits, ask students to stretch out their arms on either side and stand no closer to the next student than where their fingertips touch (If there is not enough room for this, simply remind students they cannot touch anyone else); (2) The yarn may be raised no higher than one's shoulder at any given time.
- Children can self-select when to take their turn; this supports the child who needs additional time to process the question and to formulate an answer. Some children may benefit from hearing a few answers first, to get an idea of what they want to contribute.
- This strategy lends itself to a classroom with children of differing strengths.
- The community building aspects of this strategy provide appropriate social skill cues and practice for children who might benefit from them.
- Some children are able to express themselves verbally better than they can in writing. The Spider Web benefits these students and provides the teacher with another approach to check for understanding.

Vignette Sample (Third-Grade Language Arts/Literacy)

At the completion of Library Week, the teacher had the students push the desks to the side of the classroom and stand in a circle. As she took her place in the circle, holding a ball of bright blue yarn and a pair of scissors, the students eyed her with curiosity. She reminded the class that over the past month, they had the opportunity to read books of their choice. She posed the question, "What book did you particularly like, and why?" The teacher had multiple objectives for the students: to use supporting detail to explain choice; to describe this verbally; to be enticed to read other books recommended by their classmates; and to have the class consider a variety of reasons why someone might enjoy a particular book.

Once the teacher posed the question, she explained how the Spider Web strategy worked. She waited for a student to signal that he wanted to be the first to answer, and she threw him the ball of yarn, being sure to hold on to the end of the yarn. The ball of yarn was tossed from person to person, each child took a turn responding to the question, and the "spider web" slowly grew from one lone piece of yarn strung across the circle to a vivid blue web connecting each participant in the room. Students spoke freely, listened to their classmates with interest, and appeared to be involved throughout the lesson.

When the web was completed and every student had a turn, the teacher walked slowly around the circle, cutting a piece of yarn for each child to take away. Back at their desks, students were given a variety of materials to create a bookmark, with instructions to include the piece of yarn somewhere on the bookmark. Then they were asked to take out their language arts/literacy journals and write down three reasons to read a book.

The teacher reflected on using the Spider Web strategy. One of the things that she liked was the fact that once the teacher set the strategy up and asked the question, she took a secondary role. The teacher was very much the facilitator in this process. After each student took a turn, he or she looked around to see who was ready to answer next. The students used body language and facial expressions to signal that they wanted to go next, and the person who held the ball of yarn threw it to the next person.

One of the best parts for the teacher was the fact that every student had something to contribute, and the rest of the class listened. The teacher decided that at the end of her next science unit she would use the Spider Web strategy as a review for a test, realizing that it would hold the interest of the class.

Related Information And Resources

The Co-op Co-op: http://catnet.sdacc.org/articles/oj_ID247.pdf (p. 2)

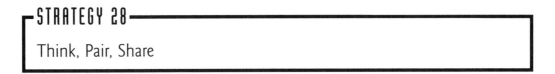

STRATEGY 28

Think, Pair, Share

Explanation

Think, Pair, Share is a learning experience that requires students to reflect and make connections to content, experience, and issues. It provides structure for a cooperative learning experience that allows all students to participate.

In this strategy, students are asked to first *think* about a question or situation and record information. Students then *pair* with another student and discuss their responses with a partner. Finally, students are asked to *share* information they have discussed together with the rest of the class.

Directions

1. Determine what objectives students will be working on and create Think, Pair, Share assignments.

2. Ask students to work on the questions or assignments alone during the *think* portion of the assignment. Students may be writing or drawing, but no one will be speaking.

3. For the *pair* segment, instruct students to discuss their responses with a partner. They may compare, contrast, and comment with one another.

4. In a teacher-led discussion, students will *share* information they've learned. Peers may add, agree, disagree, and debate.

Sample Applications

Language Arts/Literacy

- o Students make text-to-text connections.
- o Students are asked to write about their favorite character in a story or novel.
- o Students comment on a chapter conclusion or make predictions.

Mathematics

- o Students respond to a word problem.
- o Students complete a long division problem and allow partners to check and comment.

Social Studies

- ○ Students discuss new recess rules or dress codes.
- ○ Students describe presidential candidates or current events.

Science

- ○ Students discuss how to save energy at school and at home.
- ○ Students write about different scientists.
- ○ Students can respond to recall or situation questions about a science topic.

Implementation Considerations

- Teachers may decide to use timers and signals to let students know when they will transition to the next part of the strategy.

Variation: Homework

- Teachers may ask students to use a homework assignment as part of the "Think" process. For example, the teacher asks students to take out their current events reflections and hand it to their partner. Partners read each other's work during the "Think" part of the lesson and share reflections during the "Pair" part of the lesson.

How This Strategy Can Support Individuals With Learning Differences

- This strategy supports individuals with metacognitive issues as it provides a framework to think about and work with information.
- Students with a low experiential base and high aptitudes have the opportunity to share perspectives and learn from one another.
- Students with low language and social skills have the opportunity to read and discuss information in a one-on-one situation, for individual support.
- Discussion supports students with visual processing disorders.

Vignette Sample (Third-Grade Science)

In a third-grade unit on matter, the students were asked to respond to five questions:

1. *List three types of matter and give an example of each.*
2. *What is evaporation?*
3. *What is an easy way to open a jar if it is stuck?*
4. *After a rainstorm, there is often a big puddle on the sidewalk. Later, the puddle is gone. What happened to it?*
5. *Michael bought a balloon at the circus. He put the balloon in a warm place in his room. An hour later it looked a little bigger. Why did the balloon get bigger? What would happen if Michael put his balloon in the freezer?*

Each student was given a paper printed with the questions and space to respond to the questions. Students were asked to read and respond to the first question individually. They were told they could use both pictures and writing to support their answers. Then they were asked to discuss their responses with a partner next to them. Finally, students shared in a group discussion led by the teacher. The teacher found that this activity worked well and all students were engaged. It especially supported an English Language Learner because it gave her the opportunity to draw samples, like ice cubes and gas. She had a means other than language to demonstrate her understanding. Some students also drew diagrams and pictures to describe evaporation and condensation. This gave them opportunities to talk more when they were sharing with a partner and with the whole group.

Students were not evaluated on grammar and spelling, so they were more relaxed. When students discussed Question 3 with the whole class, some groups thought you should put the lid under cold water and others thought you should put it in hot water. The teacher asked students to work with their partners to find the right section in their text to support their response. This provided another student-centered "pair" opportunity for children to learn about the concept cooperatively in a constructivist learning experience. Students then shared their result with others. This activity applied science concepts to problem-solving activities. Students were able to reflect, apply, and share information.

The teacher was amazed that there was full participation during large group share when there are typically five or six students engaged in discussion. If there are only one or two hands up when he asks a question in discussion now, once in a while he will spontaneously call out, "Think!" and follow through with the Think, Pair, Share method. It always increases participation to almost 100%.

Related Information and Resources

Think-Pair-Share: http://www.readingquest.org/strat/tps.html

┌STRATEGY 29

Timeline

Explanation

Each student group researches a different time period in history and shares what they have learned with the rest of the class. Each group adds their poster to the previous one, so that at the end of all of the presentations there is a visual, sequential timeline that covers the pertinent facts in each time period. Students take an active part in the teaching, learning, and review process.

Materials

- Large poster-sized pieces of paper
- Fine-tipped markers

or

- A SMART Board

Directions

1. Choose a topic that lends itself to being divided into time periods or sequential segments.

2. Assign students to pairs or small groups.

3. Give each group a specific time period that they are responsible to research. You can provide specific questions that need to be addressed.

4. Research can be accomplished during class time, or this can be a homework assignment. You can decide how much time is needed to complete the research, depending on grade level, complexity of the topic, and class schedule.

5. Each group will create a poster board with the key facts from that particular time period in words and/or pictures. The time period in question should be written in bold letters and numbers at the top of each poster.

6. When the research is completed, each group takes a turn presenting the facts about their time period. The group that has the earliest time period goes first, and so on, and the last group will be the one that has the latest time period.

7. The visual representation is an important part of this strategy. After each group presents, they hang the completed poster in the classroom. Posters should be displayed in sequential order, starting with the earliest time period, to show the sequence of events.

Sample Applications

Language Arts/Literacy
  o Sequence of events in a novel or short story

Social Studies
  o The history of a given civilization
  o Decades in U.S. history
  o Music that was popular in the United States during different decades
  o The history of air travel
  o The history of voting, or the democratic process in the United States

Science
  o The food chain
  o The growth of a tomato plant, from planting the seed until picking the tomato
  o The growth of an orange, from planting the tree to picking the fruit
  o The life cycle of a butterfly
  o The history of computer technology
  o The steps in a science experiment
  o The stages of human development, from infancy through adulthood

Implementation Considerations

Timing

- One of the benefits of this strategy is that the children do the research and present their section of the material to their peers. Consequently, this strategy takes a minimum of two class periods, if not more.
- The strategy is introduced on Day 1. Teachers have the option to let groups do the research during the class period, using available technology, class text, or the school resource center. Alternatively, the research can be done as homework.
- After the research is complete, students will need class time to work in groups to create the timeline poster.
- The next class period or two is devoted to presentations, which can be brief or more involved, depending on the nature of the content and level of the class.

Application

- This strategy encourages higher order thinking. When the presentations are complete, you can have students look at the total scope of what has been presented and pose questions such as,

  o "What does this tell us about . . .? (What story does this tell?)
  o What themes do we see?
  o What were some of the difficulties this population had to deal with early on, and how did they overcome their adversities?
  o What is the biggest change you have seen over the years?
  o What can we learn from looking at this history?
  o How has the history of . . . influenced where we are now for this particular subject matter?

Variations

- Prepare the poster boards so that they can hook together in sequential order. Number each poster board before you hand them out to preserve the correct sequence.
- The teacher may choose to prepare an outline for students to use to take notes when listening to the other groups. In this case, have three or four questions (the same for each section of the timeline) listed on the paper for students to answer. This also guides student listening.

How This Strategy Can Support Individuals With Learning Differences

- You can choose to meet with all groups individually to provide support and check for accuracy before the group presentations.
- The timeline puts content into a cohesive whole—it shows students how something relates to what happened previously and to what followed

after. Putting material in context in this way facilitates both understanding and the memory process, as described in the information processing model in Chapter 1.

- The timeline paves the way for increased student participation. Everyone has something to contribute. Participation is accessible for all children, not just a select few.

- In class discussions, it can be difficult for some children to think of something to say before someone else does, or even to get a word in the discussion. In this strategy, the content to be shared is prepared in advance so that children know what they are going to share, and each group has their own part of the content, so there is less "He took my answer."

- A benefit of this strategy is that the students are the teachers for their section of the timeline. The students are actively involved and the teacher functions as the facilitator.

- This provides good pacing in what could have been primarily a teacher-driven lesson. The pacing of this strategy and the accompanying visual is designed to help keep students engaged.

- The completed posters, arranged in the classroom in sequential order, create an effective visual reference to help students remember the information and store it in memory so it is easily retrievable.

Vignette Sample (Fifth-Grade Social Studies/Technology)

A fifth-grade teacher was teaching a unit about explorers. He created an integrated class project with the technology teacher. He gave each group the name of an explorer and asked them to find information about the explorer including dates (in years) of exploration, route of exploration, personal background, sponsor, reason or motivation for exploration, places explored, and impact or outcomes of exploration. The explorers included Christopher Columbus, John Cabot, Juan Ponce de Leon, Hernán Cortés, Jacques Cartier, Francisco Vásquez de Coronado, Henry Hudson, and René-Robert de La Salle. In their technology class, students used the Internet to find information needed to complete the assignment. Groups of three students worked together.

When the students were ready, they had to type and print information for the timeline. Each group was given different colored paper. Students were asked to place their contributions in date order, creating a timeline on the class bulletin board. They then shared their information with the rest of the class. Discussion focused on the similarities and differences between the various explorers and the impact they had on the world, both then and now. This enabled students to relate exploration to their current experience and the geography of their own country and neighboring countries. With the timeline, the teacher pulled down the world map and students highlighted routes and lands settled. Peers were surprised to find out that many explorers shared the same interests and desires for exploration, and many met terrible fates and hardships. Putting it all together helped students see "the big picture."

Upon reflection, the teacher decided that next time he would assign cooperative learning roles to students, such as investigators and typists, or separate tasks into date finder, route of exploration investigator, studier of impact, and so on. There were enough tasks in each group to keep students busy for three periods of instruction in Social Studies and Technology.

The third day was dedicated to sharing. In this school, laptops are brought into the classroom for Technology class. The Technology and Social Studies teachers assisted with educational websites and helped students navigate the web and sort and analyze information.

The timeline strategy, in this case, was used to introduce new material and a new unit of information to the class. Once the timeline was developed, it was left on the bulletin board for reference and review and reinforcement in later instruction. It was a successful constructivist approach to introducing new information without lecture, and it held the attention of the students.

STRATEGY 30

Two Truths and a Lie (with variations)

Explanation

This is a common parlor game that works beautifully as a teaching and learning strategy. Students have to come up with three facts about a topic, and classmates have to guess which two are true and which one is false.

Materials

- Pencils
- Paper

Directions

1. Model the activity by giving students three "facts" about yourself and asking them to guess which of the three is the lie.

2. Assign students to groups of three, preferably with others they do not know very well.

3. Give students a few minutes to think up two facts about themselves that are true and something that is false. Encourage them to come up with facts that most people in the class would not know. (You may choose to remind the class to come up with facts that are "school appropriate" and are okay to share with others.)

4. Working in their groups, students take turns telling the facts about themselves and having their group mates guess which one is not true. This is frequently accompanied by laughter.

5. When all groups have finished, you can lead a brief discussion (What did you learn that was most interesting? What was the hardest to guess? Did anyone stump everyone in their group?).

6. After the first round is completed, explain that they are going to do the same process a second time, but instead of using facts about themselves, they will be working with facts about a topic the class is currently studying.

7. Choose the topic that the questions will focus on. Each student writes down three things related to the topic, two that are true and one that is false, and group mates have to guess which one is false.

8. At the end of the session, each group turns in a sheet that lists all the facts they have decided are true and the ones that they have deemed to be false.

9. If time allows after all the groups have completed their work, you can have each group pose their most difficult list to the whole class. A group discussion can clarify any questions the students might have.

Sample Applications

Language Arts/Literacy

- ○ Reading: Children think of two things that happened in the story that the class read and one that did not happen.
- ○ Vocabulary: Students write down three words and their definitions, one of which is incorrect.
- ○ Antonyms and synonyms
- ○ Grammatically correct and incorrect sentences

Math

- ○ Math facts (addition, subtraction, multiplication)
- ○ One child names three pairs of equivalent fractions and the others choose the pair that is not correct.

Social Studies

- ○ Each student writes down three states and their capitals, two that are correct and one that is wrong.

Science

- ○ Examples of the five senses, two correct and one incorrect
- ○ Living and nonliving things
- ○ Animals and their habitats

Community Building

- ○ List three of your favorite foods.
- ○ List three things you do in your spare time.
- ○ List three places you have visited.
- ○ List three activities you like to do in your free time.

Implementation Considerations

- • This can be an effective alternative to whole class presentations when the content to be covered is on a smaller scale. Each student can be required to research something specific and then share that information with her group.
- • Requiring students to work in small groups and to listen carefully and guess which statement is correct enhances student engagement and provides listening skills practice.

Variation: The Battle of the Groups (Upper Elementary)

1. Each group is given two pieces of paper, one to write the questions on and one to record answers.

2. On the first sheet, they write their group number on the top line and then list three "facts" about the content; two facts will be true and one will be false.

3. Groups are encouraged to refer to their books when writing the facts.

4. When finished, the teacher gives a signal and everyone passes their list to the group on the right.

5. Each group now has a new set of facts in front of them. Groups figure out which fact is false and write it on their answer sheet next to the number of the group that posed the question. (This is important when it comes to checking answers.)

6. Groups pass lists around until every group has answered every question. Remind groups to record answers as they work.

7. When the class is finished, the question sheets are returned to the group that wrote the question.

8. To check answers, each group takes a turn to read aloud what they wrote and calls on another group to tell which facts are true and which are not.

This variation is effective as a pre-writing strategy, for example, when students have been assigned to write an essay. This can serve as a structured brainstorming session in which all students have the opportunity to participate. Students will have to write down two things that are important for them to include and one thing that they can leave out. After they have written down their answers, they share with their classmates. Another possibility is to use this process to start a position paper, and have students write down two facts that support one side of the issue and one fact that supports the other side.

How This Strategy Can Support Individuals With Learning Differences

- This strategy provides the opportunity for students to interact with a variety of different classmates, to take turns, and to listen to each other. This presents a more structured situation in which to practice and reinforce appropriate social interaction.
- This strategy is effective for the child who does a better job explaining things verbally than in writing.
- Two Truths and a Lie supports children with visual processing concerns for the same reason: because the strategy is primarily oral and auditory.
- The pacing of the lesson, the opportunity for individual creativity, and the chance to talk with classmates all have a positive effect on student attention and engagement.

Vignette Sample (Fourth-Grade Social Studies)

In a fourth-grade Social Studies class, students were asked to discover information about their home state of New Jersey. Each student was given a county to research information related to history, economics, government, recreation, geography, and interesting facts. Students were placed in groups of three. Each student in the group was assigned a different county. To learn how to use the Two Truths and a Lie strategy, the students shared personal information. Lots of laughter and hearty conversation ensued.

Then the teacher asked students to create two truths and a lie about the county they researched. Some students moaned when they learned this fun activity was now going to mean work. Interestingly enough, the hearty laughter and conversation developed again! Kids had fun learning that Edison, New Jersey, in Middlesex County is named after Thomas Edison, and President Grover Cleveland was born in Caldwell, New Jersey. The famous Disney actress Ashley Tisdale, not actor Zac Efron, was from Neptune, New Jersey, in Ocean County! They also learned you can get the biggest blueberries in Burlington County and if you want to see the real streets from the Monopoly Game, go to Atlantic City in Ocean County.

Each group had a chance to share interesting facts and create silly fiction about their county. After the first discussion of shared information, the teacher kept the same groups and asked students to focus on specific information such as the economics or recreation of their county. In this way, the teacher was able to ensure that important information was included and discussed. Although the teacher graded each report separately, this gave an opportunity for students to share information in a fun, interactive way. Often when groups complete projects, they take turns sharing in front of the class. Although more information might be presented, there is frequently less student engagement and less listening. After a while, it often seems like only the presenting group is interested and class behavior can become an issue. With Two Truths and a Lie, students remained interested and engaged in the sharing process.

Related Information and Resources

Forsten, C., Grant, J., & Hollas, B. (2002). *Differentiated instruction: Different strategies for different learners.* Peterborough, NH: Crystal Springs Books.

Hollas, B. (2007). *Differentiating instruction in a whole-group setting.* Peterborough, NH: Crystal Springs Books.

Two Truths and a Lie: http://www.teachersfirst.com/content/knowyou3.cfm

Two Truths and a Lie Ice Breaker Activity: http://k6educators.about.com/od/icebreakers/qt/ibtwotruths.htm

---

STRATEGY 31

Venn Hoops

Explanation

Venn diagrams are often used in different content areas to help students compare and contrast information. Using the same visual concept with hula hoops and sentence strips creates a kinesthetic twist to this commonly used strategy.

Materials

- Hula hoops (two per group)
- Sentence strips
- Markers

Directions

1. Place students in cooperative groups.

2. Give each group a hula hoop, sentence strips, a marker, and labels for comparisons.

3. Ask students to create the Venn diagram shape with the hula hoops.

4. Tell students to write on the sentence strips the similarities and differences between the concepts they are comparing.

5. Have the students place the sentence strips inside the appropriate part of the Venn diagram (hula hoop).

6. Once groups have completed their Venn diagram, students can share their information with one another.

7. As students discuss their ideas, if they disagree with one another, they can move sentence strips around to redesign the diagram.

Sample Applications

Language Arts
- o Compare characters, stories, or a book vs. the movie

Social Studies
- o Presidents
- o Types of government
- o Explorers

Science
- o Compare rock types
- o Compare land formations
- o Compare seasons

Implementation Considerations

- Cut sentence strips to size to place in the hula hoops.
- Teachers must practice using hula hoops and sentence strips to make sure they fit easily in the hoops.
- Space in the classroom can also be an issue. You need to assess the space in your environment to know what furniture needs to moved to allow students enough room to work on the floor with hoops. This will help you determine the number of groups you are able to accommodate and, therefore, the number of children per group.
- There needs to be enough space for students to work on the diagrams on the floor and to walk around viewing and discussing the other Venn diagrams.

How This Strategy Can Support Individuals With Learning Differences

- Teachers can give student groups high- or low-level concepts to compare and contrast, based on academic level.
- Students can choose to draw or write information in hoops, based on ability.
- Students can choose to pair up to create sentence strip information, providing additional support as needed.
- Students can use classroom resources as needed or suggested by the teacher.

Vignette Sample (First-Grade Science)

While studying a chapter on seasons, to show students how a Venn diagram worked, the teacher used the chalkboard in a guided practice to compare spring and summer. She drew the interlocking circles on the board and wrote in student responses.

Then, the teacher separated the class into four groups of four. They were asked to move their desks and sit on the floor. Students eagerly awaited her directions. She then explained each group would use hoops and sentence strips to compare winter and fall using a Venn diagram they could touch. Using one student group, she displayed how to place the hoops in a Venn diagram shape. She asked one student for an example of how the seasons are alike. Sammy said, "You need a jacket in spring and summer." She asked Sammy to write down his answer on a sentence strip. She told the class that they could use words or pictures on their sentence strips. The next question was "How are these seasons different?" Tara said, "It only snows in winter." Tara then drew a picture of snow on the sentence strip and placed in the appropriate part of the diagram labeled "winter."

The teacher asked whether there were any questions before they began, and one student asked, "Can we only draw or do we have to write?" The teacher said it was their choice. As students retreated to work together on the Venn hoop strategy, the teacher walked around the room assisting Venn structures and probing student responses. The teacher gave a five-minute warning of the end of the Venn creation and rang a bell, calling "time" after the five minutes passed. Two groups were then asked to each walk over to another group, creating two groups of eight. The teacher asked students who had just joined the group to review and check whether the answers in the diagrams were correct. Together, group members could decide to change an answer by removing or moving a sentence strip until everyone was satisfied with the responses.

The groups were then asked to do the same review with the student group they had not already shared with. If they wanted, they could add strips from the other group to make their own Venn diagram more complete. The teacher reviewed the responses from two groups at a time. She asked whether any changes were made. Two groups said no, and the other two said they argued over the scarves being used for fall and spring, and one student argued it could snow in the fall, too, because she saw snow in November once.

The teacher noticed that students were on task and interested in the activity. She did not assign roles, but as she walked around, she asked students to take a turn contributing to at least one sentence strip. This experience laid the foundation to use Venn hoops in the future. A few weeks later, she used the same activity to compare rocks they collected on a nature hunt on school grounds while learning about rock classifications in science.

Source: Sue Ellen McConville, teacher educator, Rider University, Lawrenceville, NJ (personal communication, July, 2010).

STRATEGY 32

Walking in Their Shoes

Explanation

This strategy requires students to consider a given situation from the point of view of a character, animal, or historical figure that they have been learning about. It provides the opportunity to delve into the thought processes of that character and compare how different people see things in different ways. This is an effective way to pair academic content with character education in a meaningful way.

C. M. Charles (2011) describes how Jane Nelsen and Lynn Lott include a section on separate realities in their classroom meeting structure. The purpose of exploring separate realities is to encourage children to realize that people are different and that not all people think the same way.

Materials

- Slips of paper or small index cards
- Pens or fine-tipped markers
- Paper bag
- Background information in the form of class notes, completed graphic organizers, text, hand-outs, and/or books

Advance Preparation

1. Prepare enough index cards to have one for each child or pair.

2. On each index card, write the name of one character, animal, or historical figure from the unit or story the class has recently finished.

3. Put the index cards in a paper bag.

Directions

1. Ask each child or pair to pick a card from the paper bag.

2. Pose a question or scenario, and ask the children to approach it from the point of view of the name on their index card. The children will have to consider how "their person" would approach the given situation.

3. Give time to work on the answers, if needed. Each child or pair then shares with the class.

4. To streamline this strategy for younger grades or less complex content, describe a scenario and let children take turns picking from the bag and explaining how that character would respond. After four to six people have taken a turn, describe a new situation and give other students a chance to choose a name from the bag and respond.

5. The follow-up questions focus on the theme of multiple perspectives. The class can discuss why and how different characters, animals, or people would approach the same situation in totally different ways.

Sample Applications

Language Arts

For a story the class has read, pose one of the following:

o How would your character solve a problem?
o How does your character feel about . . . ?
o If someone was going to buy a present that your character really, really wanted, what would it be?

Social Studies

o Explorers
o People from different countries or from different periods of history
o Civil War: a soldier from the North, a soldier from the South, a plantation owner, a factory worker, President Jefferson Davis, President Abraham Lincoln

Social Skills

Each student is given one of following roles to play and is told to describe, in character, how he or she is feeling on the night before Thanksgiving:

o The turkey
o A person who has to cook dinner for lots of people and has not finished shopping and all of the food stores are closed
o A six-year-old who is going to the Thanksgiving day parade for the first time
o Children who are going to see their favorite cousins the next day
o A vegetarian

Implementation Considerations

Timing

• The timing of this strategy differs significantly according to the content and the question or situation that children are working with. Specifically, for some lessons students will be asked to talk in their groups briefly and then respond or to give answers right on the spot. In others, students may need additional time for group discussion or for additional research using the Internet or books.

Questions

• This strategy encourages students to look at situations from multiple perspectives while at the same time learning more about a particular character, animal, or historical figure. As different groups share, the class is exposed to multiple perspectives. The theme of individual differences emerges.

Variations

- Students can draw and cut out the shape of a shoe that they think their "person" would typically wear, or they can go to Google Images and print a picture of an appropriate shoe; the shoe can be paired with the oral presentation or the journal entry.
- Instead of having the students share with the whole group, this can be an individual assignment; each child has to choose three characters from a list provided and use his journal to write about how each of these characters would feel, think, and/or react in the same situation.

How This Strategy Can Support Individuals With Learning Differences

- This strategy helps children to consider that different people have different points of view. This is particularly important for children who tend to be less aware of the needs and feelings of others and have difficulty understanding the concept of different perspectives.
- Adding a picture of a shoe appropriate for a given character is a more concrete representation of the concept of individual differences and further enhances the idea. Some children learn more easily when a concrete or graphic representation is included.
- This strategy effectively pairs academic content with real-life experiences. Learning increases when the content is seen in the context of real life.
- Walking in Their Shoes encourages and facilitates higher order thinking. The open-ended nature of the strategy suggests that there is no one right answer, and this allows children to take their answer to whatever level they are able to.

Vignette Sample (Third-Grade Language Arts)

Mr. W.'s third-grade class just finished reading Snow White and the Seven Dwarfs. He had the students bring their chairs into a circle and he posed the following question: "If each of the dwarfs and Snow White walked into our classroom today, what is the first thing you think they would do?"

He explained that each child in turn was going to come up and pick a name from the bag and tell how that character would react. Mr. W. had the names of each character on two pieces of paper so that two different children had the chance to discuss each one of the dwarfs and Snow White.

Sam went first and picked Sneezy. He replied, "That is an easy one. He would take one look at our classroom and start sneezing and we would not even be able to have a conversation with him to see what he thought."

Ariel picked Grumpy, and she said that he would complain about all the desks in the room and ask why there was not a desk for him. Then he would look at the artwork hanging from the ceiling and say that he could not see it because it was too high, and he would want to know why it was so long before lunch. Then he would storm out of the room, still complaining.

> *Juan picked Happy and explained that his dwarf would walk right in, sit next to Juan, and ask to share his crayons so that they could draw together. Happy would love the third-grade classroom and all of the children in it.*
>
> *The children continued to pick names and answer the question. Some of the answers made classmates giggle, and others made them think. When all of the cards had been picked, Mr. W. posed one final question: "All of the dwarfs, and Snow White of course, walked into the same setting, our classroom. Why did they each act differently?" An animated conversation ensued.*

Related Information and Resources

Charles, C. M. (2011). *Building classroom discipline.* Boston: Pearson Education.

┌ STRATEGY 33 ──

What's in the Bag?

Explanation

Different objects, connected to a topic or a purpose, are placed in a bag. Students reflect on the contents and their meaning, drawing inferences, creating opinions, and developing ideas from bag contents for different activities and content area instruction.

Materials

- Bag
- Assorted objects

Directions

1. Place items in bag and use as a prop for different activities.
2. Student groups each get a bag with contents and discuss their contents and respond to the given assignment.

Sample Applications

Language Arts

- o Put objects or pictures in a bag and have students draw inferences about a story. If different groups have bags of the same materials, it is interesting to see what different stories or information has been inferred from the same materials.

Writing

- o Students are asked to use items in bag to brainstorm ideas for writing. Groups may have bags with the same items in it and be asked to write a story incorporating ideas related to all the objects. Students enjoy sharing different stories about the same items at the end of the assignment.

Social Studies

o Put pictures and objects related to a time period in bags and have students create an essay or timeline of events based on the objects.

Math

o Place counters and other objects in a bag and ask students to create mathematical stories. Other groups may solve mathematical questions based on the stories.

Science

o Fill a bag with different materials for recycling. Students need to identify recycling clues and discuss how to support a healthy environment through recycling.

o Fill bags with different types of rocks, ask students to sort and label them, and then explain their decisions using the rocks for models during discussion.

Community Building/Introductions

o This is an interactive way for a teacher to introduce herself to a new class or group. Ask students or other group members to create their own bags with objects to share and discuss. Within the first few days of school, ask students to take a bag and put in five things that represent themselves, such as a photo, favorite object (e.g., toy or cell phone), and other objects that represent something about them. Have students take turns removing objects from other students' bags and infer what the object means about the student.

Variation

- Students may become more involved in this activity by creating bags of objects for other groups. This activity provides another strategy to develop or reinforce concepts for students.
- For students with varying ability levels, teachers can create bags with objects that relate to basic meaning and create simple connections.
- For introduction purposes, instead of assigning this activity, allow student 10 minutes to search through their book bags, coat pockets, and lunch boxes for clues about themselves. You may also allow them to add one picture they create about themselves. It creates a light, fun atmosphere for students who are new and nervous and helps break the ice.

How This Strategy Can Support Individuals With Learning Differences

- Physical props can support language because they provide more opportunity for individuals to speak extemporaneously.
- Objects can also identify different or new concepts for individuals with a high aptitude or low experiential base.
- Items also support those with auditory issues.

Vignette Sample (Fourth-Grade Community Building/Social Studies)

In an inclusive fourth-grade classroom, children with developmental disabilities were included in a Social Studies period to support academic and socialization goals. In mid-December, each student was asked to bring in a bag with objects related to her family holiday and discuss it. During this period, a special education and general education teacher were present. For this strategy, children's chairs were moved into a circle, and the teachers sat in the circle with their own bags to share. One teacher began the discussion, modeling the format. She talked about celebrating Christmas and sharing time, gifts, and cards with others. She then took out a Christmas card with a picture of her children and passed it around. Items shared were menorahs, pictures, ornaments, advent calendars, and so on. Everyone was interested in the stories and the items.

Students focused on the student who was speaking, and they were anxious to see what object was going to come out of the bag next. They were all also eager to touch and inspect objects as they were passed around the circle. Interestingly, of the seven included children, three had experiences from other cultures and countries. One student with Down Syndrome shared "poppers," little popping toys from England that her family still uses each New Year. She got to stand up and demonstrate, and everyone laughed and smiled when the toy popped with streamers. Then another girl who was cognitively impaired showed a picture of her and her grandparents in Australia at Christmas time. She explained it was hot and sunny there in December. The student with the English poppers commented, "Been there, done that!" Everyone was surprised when the student with Down Syndrome explained she had been to England and Australia with her parents. The most interesting was when a boy revealed a box with an egg. He said his Japanese grandparents open a box with an egg in it and eat it on New Year's Day. It was a Japanese tradition. Then he said he goes to Japan or his grandparents come to visit at this time of year.

This was a very important community experience. Not only did it give students an opportunity to share and speak extemporaneously when they held an object, but it made the typically functioning students realize the children with disabilities had traveled and done exciting things they had never experienced. They were interested in the experiences of their included peers, which created meaningful discussion and positive interaction.

Related Information and Resources

What's in the Bag?: http://www.readwritethink.org/materials/in_the_bag/index.html

---

STRATEGY 34

What Up?

Explanation

This strategy allows each student in a large group to display a sign or hand signal to respond to questions. This strategy is used for formative assessment and to keep students focused and engaged on a task.

Materials

- Whiteboard, marker, and eraser for each student

or

- Small chalkboard, chalk, and eraser for each student

If none of these materials are available, students may use fingers and hand signals.

Directions

1. Provide students with individual whiteboards or chalk boards and chalk or whiteboard markers and erasers.

2. Determine which questions you would like students to respond to. For example,
    - On a scale of 1 to 5, with 5 being the highest, respond to the following question or comment: "Did you like the story?" or "The character got what he deserved in the story."
    - Recall questions related to names, places, concepts, spelling.
    - Fill-in-the-blank questions related to content, such as, "My least favorite character is _____."
    - Questions that help students practice math facts.

3. Discussion and problem solving can be based on individual responses; students can share or explain choices.

Sample Applications

Language Arts
- Agree or disagree with questions from stories or a novel
- Identify parts of speech
- Write possessives
- Subject–verb agreement

Math
- Respond to word problems
- Respond to math fact problems
- Identify numbers as composite and prime or odd and even

Science and Social Studies
- True or false
- Agree or disagree
- Specific recall questions

Implementation Considerations

- If you do not have whiteboards or chalk boards available, fingers or thumbs up and thumbs down signals can suffice. Using such signals, you can ask true or false, agree or disagree, or scale of 1 to 5 questions.

- Teachers may make up laminated cards with Yes, No, and Maybe and cards with the numbers 1 to 5 on them. Students may store cards in plastic baggies in their desks and pull out cards throughout the year as needed.
- Typically, this strategy is used as review and reinforcement, but it may also be used as a starting place for discussion and problem solving related to controversial issues and perspective sharing.
- Typically, this strategy is used as part of lesson procedures. It doesn't take up an entire period.

How This Strategy Can Support Individuals With Learning Differences

- As students raise their boards, they face forward, unable to see anyone else's responses. This strategy allows students to respond without feeling intimidated, letting students take risks.
- Teachers reviewing responses can ask students with the correct responses to share, giving students with different functioning levels an opportunity to be successful in the discussion.
- This strategy supports students with visual processing concerns, as it eliminates the need for students to respond to many review questions on a worksheet or written test and write the answer to a problem in a small space.

Vignette Sample (Second-Grade Math)

After teaching the Math facts for the numbers from 6 to 10, Mr. K. decided the students needed more time for rehearsal and he needed more opportunities to assess learning. After distributing whiteboards and markers, he shouted out addition and subtraction facts: "7 + 6, 8 + 8, 9 + 5 . . ." He gave the students a chance to respond and hold up their boards. When all boards were up, Mr. K. asked someone to volunteer to tell the class her answer. Simone shared her response, and Mr. K. then asked others whether they agreed or disagreed. One student disagreed, so he and Simone went to the board and completed the problem, explaining their response. Jason realized he made a counting mistake and Simone was correct. Both students returned to their seats for the next question. In the second half of the lesson, Mr. K. continued with subtraction facts, too. As a final challenge, he gave the students a word problem: "If Johnny and Fran each bought a package of nine baseball cards, how many cards do they have all together?" When students had different answers, Mr. K. asked students to go up to the blackboard and show their work, drawing groups of items to count or subtract from one another.

Mr. K. was not only able to identify which students needed more practice, but that the whole class struggled with the math facts for the number 9. He also identified which students were still finger counting before they wrote responses on the board. Thus, the activity provided individual and group assessments to make specific and group lesson planning decisions.

Related Information and References

Dieker, L. (2007). *Demystifying secondary inclusion.* Port Chester, NY: Dude.

┌─ STRATEGY 35 ─────────────────────────────────┐
│   │
│ What Would It Say?   │
│   │
└──┘

Explanation

This vocabulary-rich strategy directs students to match phrases that inanimate objects might have said with the objects themselves, if these objects could talk.

Materials

- Several objects or pictures (see below)
- Sentence strips or index cards
- Pens or pencils

Advance Preparation

1. Look at your vocabulary list for the week, or the short story your class will be reading, and create a list of many different nouns.

2. Assemble several inanimate objects that represent the nouns you have come up with.

3. Alternatively, use pictures or a combination of objects and pictures.

Directions

1. Divide students into an even number of groups.

2. Each group gets a number of objects and sentence strips or index cards on which to write.

3. After holding up an object and asking whether it can talk, tell children that for today, they will pretend that these objects actually can talk. Tell children that for each object their group has, they have to write down something that they think that object might say if it could talk.

4. Children work in their groups to fill out one sentence strip for each object. Then they line up the objects and put the sentence strips in a separate pile to the side.

5. When everyone is finished, two groups change places and walk to the work space of their neighboring group. The goal is for each group to read the sentence strips that their peers wrote, and place them in front of the objects that could have said them.

6. When all the sentence strips are matched with the corresponding objects, the groups work together, first with one set of objects and then with the second set, to check answers. The group who wrote the sentence strips

checks the answers at their work station. Sometimes more than one answer might make sense, and students will need to discuss their reasons for choosing a given answer.

7. The teacher walks around to each group as they are working.

Sample Applications

Language Arts

- o Vocabulary or spelling words for the week
- o Words from the short story or chapter the class is reading
- o Science vocabulary

Social Studies

- o Unit on colonial times: Pilgrim hat, Indian tomahawk
- o Picture of Confederate or Union army hats

Implementation Considerations

- The first time this strategy is used, you may want to try it with familiar objects so students can get used to the process.

How This Strategy Can Support Individuals With Learning Differences

- This strategy includes multiple opportunities for repetition and rehearsal as students discuss each object and what it is used for in order to figure out what it might say.
- Vocabulary words are paired with concrete objects or pictures, providing visual representation, which is beneficial for a student with language concerns or a low experiential base.
- The question here, "What did it say?" is open-ended, allowing for individual creativity. This strategy encourages answers that range from concrete to the more abstract higher-level thinking, which benefits a variety of learners.
- Teachers can direct students to work as a group to decide what each object should say and elect one person per group to be the scribe to write it down. This allows students to brainstorm ideas and takes the pressure off the writing part, so that everyone can participate freely.
- This strategy supports metacognition as students have to use thinking strategies to match sentence strips their peers wrote with the correct objects.

Vignette Sample (Third-Grade Language Arts/Science)

Mrs. J. was working with her students on using descriptive language, and she wanted a strategy that she could use to help reinforce vocabulary words for her science unit on growing things. In conjunction with this unit, her class is in charge of the school garden.

To start, she divided the class into an even number of groups, and she numbered the groups 1 through 6. She explained that today, for the second part of the lesson, Groups 1 and 2 would be paired together, as would Groups 3 and 4 and Groups 5 and 6.

She began this particular lesson by telling students they were going to pretend. She held up a tennis shoe and asked students whether it could talk. When they had all shouted no, she asked what they thought it might say if it actually could talk. The children were still looking at her a bit skeptically, so Mrs. J. suggested that the shoe might say, "Let's go for a run." She saw smiles begin to appear, and Andrea shouted out, "The shoe could say that he is the right shoe and he wants to know where the left shoe is because the left shoe never stays where it is supposed to."

After hearing several murmurings of "Oh, now I get it," Mrs. J. explained what they would need to do. Each group received a bag of eight different objects. They were told to spread their objects out on the table and use the sentence strips to write a phrase or sentence that each object might say. They were to make up one phrase for every object they had.

Group 1 had a packet of seeds, an individual watermelon seed, a small green plant, a stem from a flower, a seed pod, a red carnation, a root, a watering can, plant food, a picture of a rainstorm, a small container of soil, and a spade.

Jolene took the watermelon seed and wrote, "When I am planted, I will grow into something juicy and delicious." The children continued to discuss and to write until they had one sentence strip for each object. They put all their objects in a row and made a separate pile of the sentence strips.

When they were finished, Group 1 and Group 2 changed places. Group 2 came over to the work that Group 1 did and noticed that each group had totally different objects to work with. Group 2 got busy. Tara read a slip that said, "There are too many of us crowded in this little place—I want to get out," and she immediately suggested that they place that slip in front of the packet of seeds. Her group agreed. The next one read, "I am so important the plants and flowers cannot live without me." This resulted in a discussion among group members about which of the likely candidates this one should be paired with. They decided that their plan should be to match up all the other objects and see which one was left. Mrs. J. was pleased with the strategy they used to figure this out.

After the sentence slips had been matched to the objects, Group 1 and Group 2 moved to the Group 1 work station and discussed how Group 2 matched the objects with the sentence strips. Everyone agreed on several of the answers. There were three different objects that support plant life, so there was a lively discussion as to which sentence slip went where. The two groups concluded that there were three objects that could have said the same things because they were all important to keep the plants alive.

When they finished at Group 1's work station, they proceeded to check and discuss the work at Group 2's station.

Mrs. J. walked around as the students were working. She was glad to see they were using their vocabulary to explain their choices.

STRATEGY 36

Who Am I? What Am I?

Explanation

In cooperative groups, students help one another identify specific concepts by providing clues in response to the inquiry, "Who am I? What am I?" The repetition of information supports review and reinforcement well.

Materials

A choice of one of the following:

- computer labels
- index cards and masking tape
- index cards with string necklace (i.e., index card with two holes to attach string to hang down a student's back)

Advance Preparation

1. Create a list of concepts you'd like the class to discuss.

2. Make labels or necklace cards for each student, with the name of one concept on each card.

Directions

1. Create cooperative groups of four to six students. Each group should be sitting in circle.

2. Distribute the labels to students in each group, ensuring they do not see what label they receive.

3. Once students have their labels, ask them to reveal them to their groups without looking at their own label.

4. The first student in a group begins by asking, "Who am I? What am I?" The group gives hints until the student guesses correctly. Students have 10 chances to guess who they are. If they don't identify their label correctly, the group can tell them.

5. The next student takes a turn until in the group finishes.

6. When all students have identified their labels, begin sharing and closure.

Sample Applications

Language Arts

- Parts of speech: adjective, adverb, noun, verb
- Characters from a story or novel

Math

- Symbols: equal, greater than, less than, infinity, not equal to
- Vocabulary: factors, dividend, quotient, remainder

Science

- Parts of a flower
- Parts of the water cycle

Social Studies

- American Revolution topics such as the Boston Tea Party and Crossing the Delaware

o   Branches of government
o   Types of government

Implementation Considerations

Timing

- If time allows, teachers can create more than one round of terms for students.
- Provide an activity for groups who finish before the others.

Design

- If students in groups need more information about a label, they may use classroom resources, such as texts, computer, or notebooks.
- Students may begin with the question, "Who am I? What am I?" and then continue to ask questions, beginning inquiries with "Who?" or "What?"

How This Strategy Can Support Individuals With Learning Differences

- Teachers can choose high and low concepts according to student ability.
- Teachers can use pictures and words, or teachers can pre-teach and review lists of concepts with specific students or groups as needed.

Vignette Sample (Fourth-Grade Language Arts)

The students were reading the novel James and the Giant Peach, *by Roald Dahl. In a lesson on characterization, the teacher made labels with different characters from the novel, including James, Spider, Centipede, Silkworm, and Aunt Sponge. She put students in four groups of five, mixing students with high and low abilities. The lower students had the label of James, the easiest character to identify from the story. Students took turns asking "Who am I? What am I?" until they all guessed the character on their label.*

Time allowed for the next set of characters from the book, Earthworm, Glowworm, Old Green Grasshopper, Ladybug, and Aunt Spiker. The class repeated the strategy with new names.

The class was lively and enjoyed engaging in the activity. When each group was finished, they were asked to complete a worksheet with names and characteristics of the characters. Students could work with their group members or alone. Both students and teacher loved the engagement of this learning experience, and students performed very well on future assignments and activities related to characterization. In a follow-up matching and short essay quiz, students clearly identified characters and character traits from this novel.

STRATEGY 37

52 Things to Do

Explanation

Students in groups are asked to select cards from a pile and share different amounts of information about a topic based on the number on the card.

Materials

- Deck of cards for each group

Directions

1. Select cooperative learning groups and the topic or lesson objective for the strategy.

2. Place groups in a circle, and place the deck of cards in the center.

3. Name a topic, and then ask a student to choose a card from anywhere in the deck.

4. Depending on the number chosen, the students provide the rest of the group with that number of facts about the topic. Face cards are worth 10 and Aces are worth 1.

5. A student may provide as many or all of the answers individually, or he or she may call on a friend in the group as a "help line" to discuss and share until they have met the card number.

6. The game continues until everyone has had a turn to choose a card.

7. One student cannot be used as more than two help lines.

Sample Applications

Language Arts

  o Punctuation marks
  o Parts of speech
  o Grammar rules

Math

  o Math facts with a specific number (e.g., multiplication facts with the number 6)

Social Studies

  o Information about the Civil War or current events

Science

  o Information about reptiles or rocks

How This Strategy Can Support Individuals With Learning Differences

- Student partners create support for students who need it.
- If students are grouped heterogeneously, the teacher may select only low numbers on cards for students who may have trouble explaining or identifying many concepts at one time.
- The teacher may select topics for high and low functioning students accordingly.
- This strategy provides an opportunity to support turn taking, listening skills, and appropriate social interactions.

Vignette Sample (First-Grade Reading)

Ms. Q. is teaching phonics, specifically letter blends and vowel sounds. After dividing students into three groups of five, she presents a deck of cards to each group. She explains they are going to play a game called "52 Things to Do" because there are 52 cards in every deck.

Ms. Q. then calls out one student from each group and asks him or her to choose a card from the deck. Then, she calls out, "Words with short A sound." Students are asked to share their cards with the group and begin listing words with the short A. If they get one wrong, the group checks it and doesn't count it. Ms. Q. reminds all students they can call on a help line if they need it. The next three names the teacher calls "randomly" are higher functioning students. She says, "Words with the CH sound." The students choose a card and the process begins again, with the reminder of a help line as needed. One student who pulled a Jack from the deck can't name 10 "CH" words. After naming four, he calls on a help line who can only name two more with him. Finally, the rest of the groups help out, until 10 words with CH are named successfully. Other long and short vowel sounds and the BL and CK letter blends are used.

The entire period, the class is alive with laughter and eager participation. Shrieks of "Whoaaa" can be heard as children select high cards, and comments like "Easy!" and "Lucky!" are heard when children select Aces and twos. Ms. Q. never moves on and calls new names until each group has completed their round and can share their responses with the rest of the class. Calling names helps Ms. Q. create appropriate high and low questions for different student abilities. Student engagement is high and positive throughout the "52 Things To Do" strategy.

PARTICIPATION PROMPTS

Active learning strategies provide opportunities for students to be engaged in the learning process. Discussion and problem solving may be very simple and obvious active learning strategies in the general education classroom, but in an inclusive classroom, they can be challenging at times. Full class discussion is often hindered because of diverse student academic and emotional characteristics. Often, students with high academic abilities are more confident responders, sometimes intimidating lower-level academic learners. Students with social skills issues can either be too zealous or too reluctant to participate. Children who have communication issues, or have problems with auditory processing and take more time to understand the question and then formulate an answer, may not be able to assimilate the discussion quickly enough to add their own comments. Thus, classroom discussion meant to enhance and enrich learning through the sharing of ideas, perspectives, and decision making can often be skewed based on limited or inappropriate participation.

In an effort to level the playing field by inviting more students to participate in the active learning process through discussion, the following strategies support appropriate and full discussion in the inclusive classroom. These strategies—Conversation Cues, Conversation Cards, and The Whip—reinforce the spirit of inclusion because the emphasis is *to include*.

┌─ STRATEGY 38 ─────────────────────────────────

Conversation Cues: Talking Tickets and Talking Circles

Explanation

These strategies support the reluctant or the overzealous student by creating opportunities for appropriate participation in class discussion and activities. These strategies may be used together or separately.

The reluctant participants, often shy and sometimes anxiety ridden, can be provided with a cardboard circle. One side is green, signaling the student would like to participate. The other side is red, signaling the student does not want to speak. The overzealous students are provided with a limited number of talking tickets, which are handed in each time they participate in the discussion.

Materials

- Roll of tickets
- Cardboard
- Green and red construction paper

Advance Preparation

1. Cut off a strip of five tickets for each student.

2. Cut out a cardboard circle the size of the bottom of a mug. Paste red construction paper on one side and green construction paper on the other.

Directions

Talking Tickets

1. Provide each students with a strip of five tickets. Explain to the students that they can only raise their hand five times during the lesson, using one ticket each time they participate in the discussion.

2. Remind students that they must think before raising their hands to determine the best use of their tickets.

3. If students have raised their hand and are called on, they must hand in their ticket to the teacher. The teacher provides positive feedback accordingly.

4. Students who use all their tickets with appropriate questions and responses may be rewarded with a high participation grade or points toward a token economy.

Talking Circles

1. Provide students with the talking circles that you constructed.

2. Tell students that instead of raising their hand, they may flip the card over to signal green ("Yes, I want to respond") or red ("No, I do not want to respond").

3. Call on students for discussion based on their circle signals.

Sample Applications

- Tickets and circles can be used for any class discussion, to encourage appropriate participation.

Implementation Considerations

- You may use one strategy at a time or both of them simultaneously.
- The number of tickets can change depending on class needs.

How These Strategies Can Support Individuals With Learning Differences

Both

- The strategies support appropriate social skills and students with emotional needs.
- Teacher can pre-teach information to lower academic functioning students and students with anxiety issues.

Talking Tickets

- This strategy helps those students who cannot control their enthusiasm and often beg to be chosen by waving their hands wildly, even when they have little or nothing relevant to say, by encouraging them to make appropriate participation choices.
- Teachers may decide to give tickets only to the students who need them.

Talking Circles

- Talking circles enable students who are reluctant to respond and/or suffer from anxiety in groups to quietly signal to the teacher if they are ready to participate.
- When students turn the circles over, they signal to the teacher that they would like to answer the question without being embarrassed or pressured by being called on or watching students eagerly raise their hands.
- This strategy supports students with auditory processing issues because it affords them the opportunity to process discussion questions and formulate an answer before the teacher calls on them.
- This strategy provides needed response time for students with language issues.

Vignette Sample (First-Grade Social Studies)

Ms. M. was covering a science unit on living and nonliving things. One student, Maggie, was quite a reluctant participator who sometimes stuttered when nervous. Ms. M. talked about living and nonliving examples with Maggie during a reading conference earlier in the day, to pre-teach some of the science concepts. She also explained to Maggie she could use the talking button (the red/green circle) to signal Ms. M. when she would like to speak during the science class discussion later that day. In their reading conferences, Mark and Sam were each given a strip with five tickets. Mrs. M. explained to these students that it is important to think about what they would like to say before raising their hand. To help Mark and Sam make good decisions about participating in the discussion, she would give them five chances to speak during science period later that day. Each time they participated, the boys would have to give one ticket to Mrs. M. She reminded them they only had five turns to speak, so they should make their choices wisely. The boys were actually very excited about the new challenge.

In the afternoon, before Ms. M. started the science lesson, she quietly reminded Maggie, Sam, and Mark to use their discussion cues during this period. When the discussion began and Ms. M. asked who knew the difference between a living and a nonliving thing, Mark and Sam immediately put their hands up, wildly calling, "Me, me!" Ms. M. reminded them they couldn't use their tickets if they were calling out. When they quieted down, she chose Mark, who answered the question correctly. She said, "Nice job," taking a ticket away. After about five minutes of discussion, Ms. M. used an example she had discussed with Maggie earlier in the day. "Is a desk a living or nonliving thing?" she asked the class. Maggie slowly turned her circle over and waited. The teacher called on Maggie, who answered, "Nonliving," without stuttering. "Well done!" stated Ms. M. At the end of the lesson, Maggie had participated two more times and both boys answered only five questions each. Eliminating the opportunity for Sam and Mark to respond continuously and dominate class discussion enabled others, like Maggie, to have an opportunity to contribute.

STRATEGY 39

Conversation Cards

Explanation

This is a quick strategy to make any group discussion more inclusive, allowing everyone an opportunity to participate and, at the same time, keeping the focus on listening to what others are saying. This is a simple way to help children take turns and listen to their classmates.

Have you ever been in a small group conversation in a social situation? The discussion is interesting and moving quickly, and you are just waiting for a break in the chatter so that you can be heard and get your point across. The focus becomes listening for the lull in the conversation, as opposed to really listening to what other people are saying. Or, you decide not to bother trying to say something because it is too hard to get a word in edgewise. Children in the classroom can experience this as well, which is the impetus behind Conversation Cards.

Materials

- Sturdy paper (construction paper, file folders, index cards, cardboard, etc.)
- Magic markers
- Small stick-on numbers (optional)
- Laminating machine (optional)

Advance Preparation

1. Cut five rectangles from sturdy paper to make the cards. The cards should all be the same size and large enough to easily hold in one hand.

2. Using a dark-colored magic marker, number the cards from 1 to 5.

3. Alternatively, you can use foam stick-on numbers. These have the added advantage of increasing sensory input and providing tactile input for children with low vision.

4. You have the option of laminating the cards so they last longer.

Directions

1. The setting is a whole class discussion. Several students are raising their hands, looking for a chance to speak. One student is talking, and still the hand-raising persists (sometimes with accompanying groans).

2. The teacher says "hands down" to the hand raisers, gives up to five children a numbered card, and explains that this is the order in which they will have their turn to talk. She says that for the next question, other students will get cards and have a turn. The teacher takes back the cards after each round of questions so they can be reused.

3. The discussion proceeds with several children taking their turns. When the next question comes up, if the teacher sees some hands raised, she can give the same cards to the next group of students. (These do not have to be used after every question, only as needed.)

4. The first time you use this strategy, you can explain it to the class in advance, using the example of a bakery, ice-cream shop, or other local store that gives patrons tickets upon entering to secure their place in line.

5. A possibility is to take pictures of a local shop to illustrate the ticket machine. Explain that once students have their cards, their job is to listen to what others are saying. Students who did not get one of the first set of cards will get their turn within the next few questions.

Implementation Considerations

Grouping

- This strategy lends itself to both large group and small group discussions.

Applications

- Use in discussions when everyone wants to share at once (e.g., with questions such as "What is something that you do nowadays that children in colonial times would not be able to do?").
- This can be used to support instruction through discussion in any content area. Conversation Cards are most useful when you are asking children to relate content to their own lives.

How This Strategy Can Support Individuals With Learning Differences

- The cards tell children who have issues with impulsivity when their turn will be. They have something tangible to hold as a visual and sensory reminder, and it can minimize calling out or interrupting others.
- Children who have auditory processing issues may have difficulty following a discussion and trying to get the attention of the discussion leader at the same time, particularly when auditory processing is compromised. Once students know when their turn will be, it can make it easier for them to focus on discussion content.
- Children who have limited sight or who have difficulty with social cues are provided with a structure to the class discussion, which is particularly useful for individuals who cannot use visual cues to figure out when to jump into a conversation.

Sample Vignette (Fourth-Grade Social Studies)

Mrs. P. asked what children of today can do in their free time that children in colonial times did not do, and she called on Sam first. As he was talking, four other children raised their hands. Two of them had their hands raised tentatively, Marcus was making sounds with his arm in the air, and Arthur was waving his hand so furiously that Mrs. P. could have sworn he thought she asked who would like to win an iPod or an iPhone (or a pony). It appeared that Marcus and Arthur were far more focused on getting the attention of the teacher than on learning (anything) from what their classmates were saying.

Mrs. P. had introduced the Conversation Cards strategy the week before. She calmly said, "Hands down," passed out the conversation cards, and said, "Let's listen to Sam first, and then we will hear from Jamie, Marcus, Andrea, and Arthur, in that order." Discussion resumed.

One of the benefits that Mrs. P. had noticed since handing out conversation cards was that both Arthur and Marcus seemed to have a better understanding of the content covered in class discussions.

Andrea, a student in the same class, is 9 years old, has a puppy, loves music, has three very best friends, and has limited sight. Fourth grade is going well for her. Mrs. P. realized early on that she had to reflect on how she typically delivered instruction. At the beginning of the school year, Mrs. P. made up conversation cards using heavy cardboard and foam stick-on numbers. She explained the strategy to the class.

During a particularly lively discussion about current events, Mrs. P. surveyed all of the raised hands. She said, "So many of you have something to contribute today. We will start with the first five, and then I will give conversation cards to the next set of students." As she handed out the cards, she said the child's name and the number of his or her turn. Andrea was third, and she heard that she went right after Juan, who was second. Her card had a raised number as a tactile reminder, and when Mrs. P. asked for the third speaker, Andrea was ready to share.

A couple of weeks later, Andrea and her parents were meeting with Mrs. P. Andrea mentioned that one of the things she particularly liked about her fourth-grade year was that it was so easy for her to participate in class discussions. She always knew whose turn it was to speak and who she was to follow, so it made her less self-conscious about speaking up. Mrs. P. made a mental note to pass this strategy on to Andrea's fifth-grade teacher.

┌─ STRATEGY 40 ─────────────────────────────┐

The Whip

└───┘

Explanation

This is a simple strategy that provides everyone with the opportunity to speak. The teacher poses a question and then "whips" around the room, giving each child in order a chance to answer if he so chooses.

Directions

1. Pose one question, or ask students to give an example related to the content that has just been covered. Choose an open-ended question that everyone can answer in his or her own way.

2. Ask students to respond in three sentences or less. This is an important part of the process to keep the discussion moving.

3. One student can volunteer to go first, or you can choose the person who starts. After the first person speaks, the person to her right goes next. Each person in order takes his or her turn. All students know when it will be their turn.

4. Everyone has the option to say "pass" if they so choose.

5. You can engineer who speaks first, in the middle, or closer to the end by strategically choosing where in the circle to start.

Sample Applications

Language Arts/Literacy
- o Name a noun, verb, adjective.
- o What was your favorite part of the novel?
- o Which character could you most relate to, and why?

Math
- o Name something in the shape of a circle, square.
- o Give an example of one way you have used fractions in your life outside school.

Any Subject
- o What did you learn today that was most interesting or that you did not know before?

Implementation Considerations

Timing

- This works well as closure at the end of a class period and can be adapted easily to a limited time period.
- This can be used frequently throughout the school year.

Design

- The student who has more difficulty with the content or struggles a bit to answer questions can be kept near the beginning of the "whip" so that her answer is not "taken" by someone else.
- The student who has difficulty with auditory processing and needs time to first process the question before he can formulate the answer can be seated near the middle or end of the circle.

How This Strategy Can Support Individuals With Learning Differences

- This works particularly well for children with auditory processing issues because they have the opportunity to hear the question, think it through, and formulate a response, and they can figure out when their turn will be so they can be prepared.
- This is also very helpful for the child who has difficulty speaking up or trying to get called on in a whole group situation, including a child who
  - has difficulty taking risks with answering questions,
  - is unsure of the content,
  - is an English Language Learner,
  - has language issues or is struggling with expressive language,
  - has a more quiet or shy personality, or
  - does not stay focused long enough to gain the (positive) attention of the teacher to get called on.
- The Whip provides a relatively risk-free opportunity for reticent children to get used to speaking up in the class.
- This also works for the child who tends to dominate a conversation; The Whip structures the time each child has to share with the group.
- For an adaptation as needed, choose an object that represents "Speaker Power." Have each child, as she finishes speaking, hand it to the person on her right, signaling that it is that child's turn to start. This provides additional practice with turn taking.
- The quick pace of this strategy supports children with attention issues.

Vignette Sample (First-Grade Nutrition)

Mrs. O. had her students move their chairs into a circle. As they were dragging their chairs, she quietly suggested where in the circle each child should sit. She reminded her class about the nutrition unit they were working on, and asked the class to tell her what a vegetable was and what a fruit was. This review of prior knowledge was geared particularly toward the children with language issues.

Then she posed the question, "Which fruit or vegetable do you like best, and why do you like it?" She explained that each child should say "I like _____ because _____" and that they had to keep their answers short because everyone was going to have a turn. She made it clear that she wanted to hear what everyone had to say, but that children who did not want to speak were allowed to say, "I pass."

Mrs. O. decided to start with John, and she handed him a small beanbag and told him to answer the question and to remember to keep it short. John said, "I like apples because they are crunchy." The teacher reminded him to pass the beanbag to Samantha, on his right, because it was now her turn to talk. She said, "I like strawberries because red is my favorite color," and she passed the beanbag to the boy on her right, who gave his answer.

The beanbag made its way around the circle, and everyone had a chance to share. Only one child asked to pass and then changed her mind immediately as she thought of an answer.

Mrs. O. was particularly pleased because everyone answered the question, even the children she rarely heard speak aloud in class. One of her concerns as an inclusion teacher was how to fully include all children, how to literally give everyone an opportunity for his or her voice to be heard. She felt that using The Whip was one small but effective step in this direction.

CHAPTER 4 SUMMARY

- Active learning strategies provide opportunities for the learner to be the focus of the learning process, individually or in groups.
- Active learning strategies have to be tied to academic content and appropriate standards.
- Forty strategies to promote active learning are presented alphabetically. (To easily reference which strategies support specific learning needs, see Figure 2.3 in Chapter 2.)
- Each strategy is presented with clear descriptions and examples under these headings: Explanation, Materials, Advance Preparation, Directions, Sample Applications, Implementation Considerations, and How This Strategy Can Support Individuals With Learning Differences.
- Vignettes that share real-life implementations of the strategies are provided at the end of each strategy.

5

The Journey Continues

In Chapter 1, we invited you to take a journey with us. It was our intention as authors to provide teachers with an "at your fingertips" resource to support diverse learners in the classroom. We know that no one strategy, concept, or program can meet the needs of all students, and as educators it is our professional and ethical responsibility to continually seek opportunities to identify student needs and design effective instruction to improve students' performance. We trust our explanation of active learning and its connection to student learning characteristics, with 40 specific examples, has increased your repertoire of teaching techniques and your suitcases are fuller! Remember: Teaching is an art, not a science; it is a learning experience in itself, with many trials along with the successes, hence the journey.

Our goal for this book has been to share our belief in, and our success with, active learning strategies in the classroom. Our hope for our readers is that you take our ideas and run with them, adapting the strategies to both the content you cover and to the learning needs of your students. *Use these strategies and make them your own.*

Off to our ongoing journey. The following checklist is provided to help you pack:

✓ The conviction that good teaching is good teaching, and the strength of active learning strategies is that they improve the quality of learning for everyone. They embody the best possible learning for all children: those who are classified, those who struggle with one or more subjects or who struggle on occasion, as well as those who are doing well in school and those who excel.

✓ The understanding that active learning strategies have a purpose; they motivate students and, at the same time, they are used to very clearly address state standards and academic and behavioral objectives.

✓ Your ability to take a risk, plan, and go with the flow as you use active learning strategies in your classroom.

✓ The knowledge of the strengths and needs of each of your students and how this informs lesson and strategy design.

✓ Figure 2.3 Strategies That Address Specific Learner Characteristics, in Chapter 2, as a fingertip reference.

✓ A continued appreciation for the role that reflection plays in the ongoing planning, teaching, and assessment process, keeping in mind that reflection enhances quality instruction and learning.

✓ Your sense of adventure.

✓ Your sense of humor.

✓ A friend or several (or at least their cell phone numbers or e-mail addresses); we all need someone to cheer with us for our successes and encourage us when needed.

✓ Your continued appreciation for the children you teach, for the individual and unique qualities that each and every one of them brings to the table or, in this particular case, to the classroom.

References

Bender, W. (2002). *Differentiating students with learning disabilities: Best practices for general and special educators.* Thousand Oaks, CA: Corwin.

Bender, W. (2008). *Differentiating instruction for students with learning disabilities: Best teaching practices for general and special educators.* Thousand Oaks, CA: Corwin and Council for Exceptional Children.

Benson, B. P. (2009). *How to meet standards, motivate students, and still enjoy teaching! Four practices that improve student learning.* Thousand Oaks, CA: Corwin.

Bonwell, C. C., & Eisen, J. A. (1991). *Active learning: Creating excitement in the classroom.* (ASHE-ERIC Higher Education Report No. 1) Washington, DC: George Washington University.

Brophy, J. E. (1997). *Motivating students to learn.* New York: McGraw-Hill.

Bruneau-Balderrama, O. (1997). Inclusion: Making it work for teachers, too. *Clearing House, 70*(6), 328–330.

Carroll, L., & Leander, S. (2001, January). *Improving student motivation through the use of active learning strategies* (Master of the Arts Action Research Project). (ERIC Document Reproduction Service No. ED455961)

Chapman, C., & King, R. (2003). *Differentiated instructional strategies for reading in the content areas.* Thousand Oaks, CA: Corwin.

Charles, C. M. (2011). *Building classroom discipline.* Boston: Pearson Education.

Choate, J. S. (2004). Basic principles and practices of inclusive instruction. In J. S. Choate (Ed.), *Successful inclusive teaching: Proven ways to detect and correct special needs* (pp. 2–17). Boston: Pearson.

Cook, B. G. (2002). Inclusive attitudes, strengths, and weaknesses of pre-service general educators enrolled in a curriculum infusion teacher preparation program. *Teacher Education and Special Education, 25*(3), 262–277.

Corney, G., & Reid, A. (2007). Student teachers' learning about subject matter and pedagogy in education for sustainable development. *Environmental Education Research, 13*(1), 33–54.

Dieker, L. (2007). *Demystifying secondary inclusion.* Port Chester, NY: Dude.

Dewey, J. (1926). *Democracy and education.* New York: Macmillan.

Fenwick, T. J. (2001). *Experiential learning: A theoretical critique from five perspectives.* Columbus, OH: ERIC Clearinghouse.

Forsten, C., Grant, J., & Hollas, B. (2002). *Differentiated instruction: Different strategies.* Peterborough, NH: Crystal Springs Books.

Friend, M. (2010). *Interactions: Collaboration skills for school professionals.* Boston: Pearson.

Friend, M., & Bursuck, W. D. (2002). *Including students with special needs: A practical guide for classroom teachers.* Boston: Pearson.

Friend, M., & Bursuck, W. D. (2009). *Including students with special needs: A practical guide for classroom teachers.* Upper Saddle River, NJ: Merrill/Prentice Hall.

Gable, R. A., & Hendrickson, J. M. (2004). Teaching all students: A mandate for educators. In J. S. Choate (Ed.), *Successful inclusive teaching: Proven ways to detect and correct special needs* (pp. 2–17). Boston: Pearson.

Ginsberg, M. B. (2005, July). Cultural diversity, motivation, and differentiation. *Theory Into Practice, 44*(3), 218–255.

Gregory, G. H., & Kuzmich, L. (2004). *Data-driven differentiation in the standards-based classroom.* Thousand Oaks, CA: Corwin.

Guillaume, A. M., Yopp, R. H., & Yopp, H. K. (2007). *Strategies for active teaching: Engaging K–12 learners in the classroom.* Upper Saddle River, NJ: Pearson.

Hallahan, D. P., & Kauffman, J. M. (2006). *Exceptional learners: Introduction to special education.* Upper Saddle River, NJ: Pearson.

Heacox, D. (2002). *Differentiating instruction in the regular classroom. How to reach and teach all learners, grades 3–12.* Minneapolis, MN: Free Spirit.

Hollas, B. (2007). *Differentiating instruction in a whole-group setting: Taking the easy first steps into differentiation.* Peterborough, NH: Crystal Springs Books.

Jarolimek, J., & Foster, C. (1981). *Teaching and learning in the elementary school* (2nd ed.). New York: MacMillan.

Jensen, E. (2000). Moving with the brain in mind. *Educational Leadership, 58*(3), 34–37.

Jensen, E. (2001). *Arts with the brain in mind.* Alexandria, VA: Association for Supervision and Curriculum Development.

Kame'enui, E. J., Carnine, D. W., Dixon, R. C., Simmons, D. C., & Coyne, M. D. (2002). *Effective teaching strategies that accommodate diverse learners.* Upper Saddle River, NJ: Pearson.

Karten, T. J. (2005). *Inclusion strategies that work! Research-based methods for the classroom.* Thousand Oaks, CA: Corwin.

King-Shaver, B., & Hunter, A. (2003). *Differentiating instruction in the English classroom: Content, product and assessment.* Portsmouth, NH: Heinemann.

Kounin, J. S. (1977). *Discipline and group management in classrooms.* Huntington, NH: Krieger.

Lavoie, R. (1989). *How Difficult Can This Be? F.A.T. City Workshop: Understanding Learning Disabilities* [Video]. Alexandria, VA: PBS Educational Media.

Lenz, B. K., & Deshler, D. D. (2004). *Teaching content to all: Evidenced practices for middle and high school settings.* New York: Allyn & Bacon.

Lewis, L. B., & Doorlag, D. H. (2006). *Teaching special students in general education classrooms.* Upper Saddle River, NJ: Pearson.

Mastropieri, M. (2001). Is the glass half full or half empty? Challenges encountered by first-year special education teachers. *Journal of Special Education, 35*(2), 66–75.

Mastropieri, M., & Scruggs, T. (2000). *The inclusive classroom: Strategies for effective instruction.* Upper Saddle River, NJ: Merrill/Prentice Hall.

Merriam-Webster Online. (2010). Retrieved from http://www.merriam-webster.com

Michigan Literacy Progress Profile. (2003). *K–3 training module 04.* Retrieved from http://www.mlpp-msl.net/training/default.htm

O'Shea, D. J. (1999). Tips for teaching: Making uninvited inclusion work. *Preventing School Failure, 43*(4), 179–181.

Perna, D. M., & Davis, J. R. (2007). *Aligning standards and curriculum for classroom success* (2nd ed.). Thousand Oaks, CA: Corwin.

ProTeacher Community. (2006). *Archives.* Retrieved from http://www.proteacher.net/discussions/showthread.php?t=13677

Rugutt, J. (2004, Fall). Linking individual and institutional factors to motivation: A multi-level approach. *Journal of Educational Research and Policy Studies, 4*(2), 52–85.

Salend, S. J. (2005). *Creating inclusive classrooms: Effective and reflective practices for all students.* Upper Saddle River, NJ: Pearson.

Silberman, M. (1996). *Active learning: 101 strategies to teach any subject.* Needham Heights, MA: Allyn & Bacon.

Silberman, M. (2006). *Teaching actively: Eight steps and thirty-two strategies to spark learning in any classroom.* Boston, MA: Pearson.

Sliva, J. A. (2004). *Teaching inclusive mathematics to special learners, K–6.* Thousand Oaks, CA: Corwin.

Smart, K., & Csapo, N. (2007). Learning by doing: Engaging students through learner-centered activities. *Focus on Teaching, 451–457.*

Smith, T. E. C., Palloway, E. A., Patton, J. R., & Dowdy, C. A. (2006). *Teaching students with special needs in inclusive settings.* Boston: Pearson.

Snyder, R. F. (1999). Inclusion: A qualitative study of inservice general education teachers' attitudes and concerns. *Education, 120*(1), 173–180.

Sousa, D. A. (2001). *How the brain learns* (2nd ed.). Thousand Oaks, CA: Corwin.

Sousa, D. A. (2007). *Brain research into classroom practice.* Retrieved from http://www.ldaofmichigan.org/articles/Sousa1-07.htm

Swanson, H. L. (1987). Information processing theory and learning disabilities: An overview. *Journal of Learning Disabilities, 20,* 3–7.

Tomlinson, C. A. (1999). *The differentiated classroom: Responding to the needs of all learners.* Alexandria, VA: Association for Supervision and Curriculum Development.

Tomlinson, C. A., & Allan, S. D. (2000). *Leadership for differentiating schools and classrooms.* Alexandria, VA: Association for Supervision and Curriculum Development.

Udvari-Solner, A., & Kluth, P. (2008). *Joyful learning: Active and collaborative learning in inclusive classrooms.* Thousand Oaks, CA: Corwin.

Uguroglu, M. E., & Walberg, H. J. (1979). Motivation and achievement: A quantitative syntheses. *American Educational Research Journal, 16*(4), 375–390.

Vollmer, J. R. (2002). *The blueberry story.* Retrieved from http://www.jamievollmer.com/blue_story.html

Wood, J. (2009). *Pathways to teaching strategies: Practical strategies for the inclusive classroom.* Upper Saddle River, NJ: Pearson.

Wood, K. (2008). Mathematics through movement: An investigation of the links between kinesthetic and conceptual learning. *Australian Primary Mathematics, 13*(1), 18–22.

Zmuda, A. (2008, November). Springing into active learning. *Educational Leadership, 66*(3), 38–42.

CORWIN

A SAGE Company

The Corwin logo—a raven striding across an open book—represents the union of courage and learning. Corwin is committed to improving education for all learners by publishing books and other professional development resources for those serving the field of PreK–12 education. By providing practical, hands-on materials, Corwin continues to carry out the promise of its motto: **"Helping Educators Do Their Work Better."**